"DONKEY'S EARS APART"

"DONKEY'S EARS APART"

BY

GEORGE TORODE

Author of

"Donkey's Ears Ago"

First Printed in
Paper Back
1997

Published by
George Torode
4, Rohais de Haut , St. Andrews,
Guernsey, Channel Islands.

Edited by Miss Carrie Torode, St. Andrews, Guernsey.
This book was made in conjunction with
Mr.Neil Cookson - Lancashire - Mainland -
United Kingdom.
ISBN 0 9529501 11

DEDICATION

This book is dedicated to the memory of
a man whose grin and happy disposition
was a joy every time you met him.
A Journeyman Carpenter, Husband, Father
and Grandpa.
A Friend by name, and a Friend
by Nature.

REX STANLEY FRIEND
1933 - 1993.

ACKNOWLEDGEMENTS

Neil Cookson for his encouragement, enthusiasm and all that hard work.

Carrie Torode for all her efforts at putting the punctuation right.

Kay Bragg for her excellent article on Steve Picquet.

E.V. Coltman for Birds of the Storm.

Fallaize Reprographics (Gsy) Ltd.

Ave Jelly for Fred Ruff's Photo

Carel Toms for his many informative Guernsey books, and also the Guernsey Evening Press.

PREFACE

How would you know if you qualified to read this book? Well, were you taught to swim in the childrens pool, with an old car inner tube by a smashing chap called Roy Langlois. Were you ever sent for a haircut to a barber called Otto Le Gallez? Did you ever utter that immortal phrase -- "The trouble with the bloney English is, they comes over yer, buys a plot of land, and they think they bloney owns it!" We ask deep and meaningful questions, like, "If Guernsey has no letters on car registration plates, who has still managed to get a personalized number plate?" (Answer:- ALEC FORTY).

In 'Donkey's Ears Ago' I gave an example of how children can drop you in the cart, it's still happening. Emma said, "Grandad, can you make a noise like a frog?"

"No love, I'm afraid I'm not very good at animal impressions."

"Oh - - - alright, - - -" sigh, - - - never mind then."

"You seem very disappointed!"

"I am, - - - Granny said when you croaked we could all go to Disney Land."

If you enjoyed meeting Reggie Lamb, Fred the Gas, Noel and Otto, they're here again, and new friends to meet besides. Guernsey is the greatest Island in the world, never be ashamed of being a Donkey, and always remember the Donkeys Creed:--

When we works, we works hard
and when we plays, we plays rough
and when we thinks, we goes to sleep.

I hope you enjoy this book.

THE GOOD OLD DAYS

We met, we married, a long time ago
He worked for long hours and wages were low
No telly, no radio, no bath, times were hard
Just a cold water tap and a walk up the yard.

No holidays abroad, no carpets on the floors
We had coal on the fire - we never locked doors
Our children arrived - no pill in those days
And we brought them up without the State Aid.

No valium, no drugs no LSD
We cured our pains with a good cup of tea
If you were sick you were treated at once
Not 'Fill in a form and come back next month.

No vandals, no muggings, there was nowt to rob
In fact, you were rich with a couple of bob
People were happier in those far - off days
Kinder and caring in so many ways.

Milkmen and paper boys would whistle and sing
And a night out at the flicks a wonderful thing
Oh, we had our share of troubles and strife
But we had to face it, that was life.

But now I'm alone and look back through the years
I don't think of bad times, troubles and tears
I remember the blessings, our home and love
We shared them together, and I thank God!

ANON

CONTENTS

CONTENTS

==============================
==============================

CHAPTER ONE

THE DEAR OLD STOVE AGAIN! (ORMERING TIDE)

You might remember that the old pot-bellied stove which I loved so much, was the focus of much attention in the workshop at 'Stalag Ten,' especially at lunchtimes when the regulars like Charlie, Ernie, Art, and St.Sampson's Bill, would pull the long benches around it on three sides. As an apprentice I didn't qualify to sit on the bench, so I made do with an upturned 'Snowcem' drum tucked right in the corner.

I used to love my stove duties on a winter's morning, it was a challenge to get it, not only going, but glowing by lunchtime.

It's funny, but, in the same way as you remember everyday as sunny when you were a kid, so I remember most of the winter's mornings at 'Stalag Ten' as very cold and very wet, especially 'Omering tide' day's.

For the benefit of none locals an ormer is an ear shaped univalve mollusc, hence the name, aurus maris - sea ear. A very rough description would be like a very large limpet, which is cut out of its shell, beaten tender with a wooden mallet, sprinkled with flour and fried. To us donkey's it can be described in just two words, 'Yummy - yummy' - - - or is that only one word used twice?

Anyway, to return to the workshop, old Ernies voice would sound out from the general direction of his workbench.

"Dearie me today next week, is that the time already? well bless us and save us, who'd 'ave thought we'd live to see the day? lunchtime's come 'round already," and with that, bodies would be seen leaving their benches all around the workshop, making their way to my warm cast iron baby. Soon the golden liquid was being poured from vacuum flasks.

"What time's low water then?" Bill's gruff voice would demand.

"About 3-oclock I think," Arties small voice would answer.

"Why? are you thinking of going down?"

Ernies turn this time.

"Well I thought I might go as far, and get a

feed," said Bill.

Now I should interject here to say that a feed of ormers in those days was around two or three dozen. Whereas in this day and age even half a dozen would be a positive 'banquet,' - - - - so much for progress I suppose!

"Where do you go then?" Ernie asked casually.

"Aagh -- Aagh," went Bill, with all the suspence and intrigue he could muster, "Aagh -- Aagh - - - that's for me to know," he said, tapping his index finger on the side of his nose, "That's for me to know and you to find out. - - - - pausing for maximum effect.

"Sailor Jack!" said a voice from the other side of the stove.

"Whaaat!" spluttered Bill, going a worrying shade of purple, "How do you know that?"

"I saw you there, last tide," said Georgie, with a mischievous twinkle in his eye.

"And just where were you spying from?" said Bill, cooling down a little as he realized it was Georgie that had spoken.

"I wasn't spying from anywhere," said

Georgie, "I saw you when I was motoring out through the pier heads in 'Dawn Lass' on my way to Brehon tower."

"Aagh," said Bill again, this time with a note of triumph in his voice, "Now we know where you go!"

"Good place," Georgie replied, "I've had eight dozen there in an hour."

"I've never had eight dozen anywhere in my life," said a quiet little voice from under Artie's cap.

"I'm not surprised," grunted Bill, "You've got to get wet for them, it's no good standing on dry land and waiting for them to come to you." At this there seemed to be a murmer of agreement from all assembled. Bill pressed on, "You've got to get in up to your waist and then feel under the rocks, that's where they are.

"I know, I know," said Artie sadly, "But even so, eight dozen!"

"That's nothing," said Ernie, "On a good tide down at Belgrave, just off left of the Salerie Battery, I've known to have eleven dozen."

"Only eleven?" chimed in another voice, that was it! they were off, the numbers of dozens were going up and up like an auction sale, just before they reached the realms of telephone numbers Ernie commented that it wasn't always the amount that was so important as the size, after all he said, "I've had 'em up to seven inches in length."

"Only seven!" chimed in the voice again, but this time before the numbers game could start again Georgie said, "I've seen one the size of a dinner plate." That stopped everyone in their tracks, as they looked to see if he was joking, - - - "Well the shell at least," he added.

"And where?" demanded Bill, bristling with indignation, "Might that have been?"

"Dirty Dick's," said Georgie with a grin.

"What? Fred Benham's place?"

"That's right," he smiled, "Fermain Tavern."

Fred Benham had been the landlord, and a good landlord at that, for as long as anyone could remember, but the nick-name for the place, went back even further than that, in the same way that Trafalgar Inn had become 'The Parrot.'

"Hanging on the wall in the public bar," Georgie continued, "Massive it was."

"I think," said a sleepy voice from under the cap, sounding for all the world like the dormouse, at the Mad Hatters tea party, "I think you'll find that, what you saw was an 'Abalone,' found off the west coast of America and some parts of Australia."

"Same thing," said Georgie like a flash.

"You wouldn't think so if you tried to eat one," Ernie came in, "I'll tell you one thing," he said, "If you nailed a pair of abalones to the bottom of your boots, you'd never live long enough to wear them boots out!"

Everybody laughed; I suspect that Georgie knew they were too tough to eat as well, but he loved to wind the older ones up.

"I bet," said another voice, I think it was Stan, "I bet you can't remember the name on the wooden plaque just above the shell?"

Surprised faces with arched eyebrows looked from one to another, then Georgie spoke again.

"I do," he said, "But I can't say it, I can spell it, but I can't say it," and with that he took the pencil from behind his ear, stooped to pick up an empty Bucktrouts Three Star fag packet, tore it down one side and on the plain cardboard inside he wrote, 'Wubmadiitu."

"Yes!" said Stan, "That's the word, - - never found out what it meant though, I thought that if the abalone was Australian, maybe it was an Aboriginal word."

"I wondered about it loads of times,"said Georgie,"till one night I decided to ask the barman what it meant."

He said, "Will you buy me a drink if I tell you?" By this time I was so fed up of trying to guess, that I said,"Oh go on then."

He said, "I've told you." I looked at him puzzled, then he laughed, he said, "That's what it spells -- Will U buy me a drink if I tell you."

I laughed, I said, "Go on then, it's a fair cop, what will you have."

He said, "Ahh, for that you have read it backwards. U thought I intended drinking a mild beer, wrong! I'll have a double whisky!"

Everybody laughed, "No wonder you've always remembered it," said Ernie still laughing, "If it cost you a double whisky."

"Ahh well!" said spoilsport Bill beginning to rise - - - I suppose we'll have to!" Lunch was over!

CHAPTER TWO

BARBERS AND BOXERS

In 'Donkey's Ears Ago' I referred to the Le Gallez Bros barber shop in the Bordage. I inferred that it was the kind of place your father sent you just to be spiteful, and all this just because Otto once sheared my head 'till it looked like a poodle that had lost a battle with a Combine Harvester. Well! imagine my surprise many years later, just after an article had appeared in the Guernsey Evening Press about my photographic album of Guernsey characters. I got a phone call from a nurse at a private residential home who said, Mr.Otto Le Gallez wishes to send his regards and congratulations on a splendid article, and would like you to know that if it was ever possible he would love to see your album. I asked how old Otto was at this time, and on receiving the answer '86' I said, will you please tell Mr.Le Gallez it would be an honour and a pleasure to bring it down as soon as I can. A couple of Saturdays later when I was setting off, I met an old work mate of mine, who, when I told him who I was going to visit said, "Ask him about the year he was so far in front in the church to church walk that he went into the 'Channel' (Channel Islands Hotel, now the Savoy) and had a pint and a fag, and then came out and finished the race."

When I arrived at the residential home, Otto was sitting on a bench seat on the lawn, bathing in the glorious sunshine. After the introductory formalities we started through the album, and my goodness he was sharp, he was razor sharp. Eighty six years old and he knew every face, every name, he even corrected me on one I got muddled on. I could see why he was legendary with 'bookies odds,' the speed with which he could assess 'trebles,' 'yankees,' accumulators and the like, exactly what return for what stake. One story I really like which demonstrates the sharpness of Otto's mind, involves that very greatly loved 'newsboy' and later Lottery ticket man Billy Roswell. Apparently Billy was really down one day because he wasn't able to sell many papers, and as he worked on a small commission, (probably a halfpenny per paper) he was going to have worked and walked all day with very little to show for it. Poor ol' Billy I can see him now in my minds eye shuffling along the road, his hand just touching the wall from time to time to steady himself. Touching his cap, "Hello Jim" to all the men, "Hello Missus" to all the ladies, and his two most famous phrases, "What's the score down the track" and to the girls, "Don't forget I'm coming to your house for a cup of tea." Anyway Billy was down this day and he stepped in to Otto and Nan's place. Because Billy couldn't read or write he had to rely on someone to tell him what headline to shout. Otto, learning why he was disheartened said, "Give us one of those papers here," and looking at the front page discovered the big story and photo was a big hay barn fire at a farm in St.Saviours, a lot of damage, but luckily no-one injured.

"Right," said Otto, "Now let's look inside, here we are, Births -- Engagements -- Marriages -- deaths, here we are deaths, one - two - three -four - five. Right Billy you shout, Big fire at St.Saviours -- five dead, and if anybody argues with you, you send 'em up here to me!"

I had a great afternoon with Otto, and later, when inside the home he was showing me his collection of walking race trophies, small cups, medals and certificates. I remembered the incident with the pint and fag. So I told Otto what my mate had said and asked him what year that was in. He pointed to a medal that said 'second place,' this intrigued me even more.

"You'd better tell me the whole story," I said.

"Well," said Otto, "It was the year I was in my best form ever, I had trained really hard and was several minutes quicker than my nearest rival, and so we set off on the church to church walk. I was going like a steam train that day, and when I knew I only had a few hundred yards to go to finish, I went into the 'Channel' for a pint and a smoke. I was standing out by the door for quite a while with my beer in one hand, my fag in the other, when my nearest rival finally went past. I finished my drink and still puffing on my 'ciggy,' went down and over the line -- second place!"

"But why?" I pleaded, "The one year you had the chance to be champion?"

"Well it was like this," he said, "The war was not long over, there was practically nothing in the shops, we hadn't been long married and my little wife had her heart set on a canteen of cutlery. Now just by coincidence the second prize was exactly that, so I went around the course as quick as I could to prove to myself I could have won, and then - - - - she got her canteen of cutlery. - - - - After all he added if I'd won, I'd have only had the trophy."

What a character, 'only had the trophy.' I've seen men since, who pound the road 364 days a year in training, who would kill for that trophy. - - But Otto let it all go for love.

Just occasionally we would have a couple of outsiders join us at the stove. It would happen if somebody happened to be on business at the workshop just as the clock got around nine thirty, then they would fetch their flask and sandwiches from their van or whatever and join us in some warmth and convivial conversation. One such day we had a couple of characters known as 'Digger Dave' and 'Johnny the Coal.' The digger part of Dave's name must have been a reference to his driving a J.C.B. earth mover as he did not sound Australian. As we all took up our places around the stove, which I remember, distinctly glowing red, I was clambering over to my upturned 'snowcem' drum, whilst Charlie was doing his usual trick with a toasting contraption and (up to that point in time) a perfectly good cheese sandwich.

I think that there had been boxing the night before at St.Georges hall, because that was certainly the gist of the conversation already in progress. On this particular morning the chatter was, what my Dad used to describe as, -- like a Chinese wedding, everyone talking and nobody listening.

"You've got to go back before the war for good boxers," Bill said gruffly. That stopped a few of 'em chatting.

"Blokes like 'Winkle' Perriam," there was a general murmer of approval at that one, "And his brother Les" said Charlie.

"What are you on about," growled Bill, "Les didn't box."

"Oh, didn't he," said Charlie, getting all indignant, "Oh didn't he indeed. I'll have you know Les was Royal Navy Champion at his weight."

"He's right there," Ernie said, coming into the conversation. "Royal Navy Champion for several years, some say he was as good as Winkle."

"Well I never knew that, I have to admit it, I never knew that."

"What was the name," began Charlie, in a pensive enquiring tone, "Of those two brothers with a French name?"

"Walter Gent," said Bill in his normal aggressive way, completely ignoring Charlies question, "Walter Gent, that's another one, boy he could box!"

"I heard," said Johnny the Coal, "That Walter Gent used to stand sideways in the ring."

"That's right, that's right," said Bill again, "He could deliver a devastating blow from that stance and, if you think about it, he offered very little target for his opponent to aim at, oh yes, he was a crafty boxer."

"Terrified of his missus though," said Ernie right out of the blue, he got everyones attention with a statement like that!

"What was the name of those two French boys?" Charlies voice almost pleading by now.

"Yes," Ernie continued, "My Father was talking to him outside his house at North Side just after he won the championship, and his wife came out and said," 'If you're not inside here in two minutes there's going to be serious trouble,' and as she was going back to the door, she said, 'Come on, come on, you've got the dishes to do!' My Father said, 'He gave a nervous little laugh and said, ah well I'd better go and keep the peace,' and he was off. My ol' man said, 'I'd only gone a few paces, and could hear her yelling and shouting and giving him what for!'"

"Two of them there was - - - French they were, they were good, oh what were their names?" Charlie was going dippy by this time, still no-one was taking any notice.

THE AUTHOR WITH A FRIEND, REX STANLEY

WALTER GENT THE GENTLE GIANT

JOHN 'THE CANARY' SARRE

MARY LE SAUVAGE

PHEOBIE

GEORGE STONEBRIDGE

PETER LEGG

HENRY POULLAIN

"Eh?" - - two little sleepy eyes were looking up at me from under a peaked cap.

"They're talking about Walter Gent, Art, "I said.

"Oh, him, his missus used to chase him down the street with a frying pan!" and with that he lowered his head again and went back to sleep.

"Steve Picquet!" said Bill in a triumphant voice," no ones thought of Steve, that lives in the bunker out at Pleinmont."

"Ah!" said Johnny the coal, "But I thought we were talking about donkey's."

"Well what do you think Steve is, he's been Guernsey champion!"

"No he hasn't, he's been Channel Islands Champion -- brilliant boxer! -- featherweight, he had over 200 contests but he's a Jerseyman."

"What!" Bill exploded, "Steve a Crapaud!"

"That's right," assured Ernie, taking great delight in proving Bill wrong twice in one lunch-break.

It is at this point I should explain for any non-local what the 'Donkey' and 'Crapaud' business is all about. It is a tongue-in-cheek insult exchange largely for use at the Annual 'Muratti' football match between the Islands. Although Alderney have won it once (and most people would be thrilled if they did it again), most often the final is between Guernsey and Jersey. Guernsey has frogs but no toads, when we found out that Jersey had both, we started calling out to them 'Crapaud' patois-French for toad. They found out that amongst Guernsey working men there was a long standing joke that any Guernsey man who was still single and had never been to London, was called a 'Donkey,' so we all became Donkey's. Hence at the football match, or later down at the White Rock to see the ferry leave, you'd hear an exchange:-- "We beat you Crapauds fair and square this time!" and they'd reply, "We'll beat you Donkey's next year!"

"I remember the name was French -- in fact I'm sure they were French - - two brothers the name started with -- now let me see --'B' I think."

"There's been good ones since the war as

well," Johnny the coal ventured, "What about Ken Simon the heavyweight? Rex and Bruno Ogier? the three Veron brothers -- the Lorier brothers!"

Whilst all the hub bub of conversation was going on I noticed a sly smirk on the face of Ernie, thinking back afterwards I realized he had been tormenting, or rather leaving in torment poor 'ol Charlie, right through the lunch-break purposely because in a very quiet voice, (I thought I was the only one who heard it) he said, "Branquet."

"That's it!" yelled Charlie as he leapt to his feet, in a manner usually reserved for those occasions when his cheese sandwiches turned to charcoal, "That's it! the Branquet boys, Alain and Marcel." All those who hadn't realized he'd been struggling all the lunch-break to remember their names, must have thought he was two cans short of a 6 pack!

"They were good," he said, "They were very good." It was then, whilst he was standing that he realized, not only why his sandwich had not turned to charcoal on this occasion but also, that it was very unlikely to do so having tumbled out of the toasting rack and was now laying in a mixture of paraffin, motor oil, and wood shavings on the workshop floor. I'm sure, rather than admit anything had gone wrong, if no-one had been looking he'd have brushed it off and ate it anyway. As it was he dumped it and set up another one to toast, I thought good! it means we'll get a longer lunch break whilst he's waiting.

"What about Les Collins?" said Ernie.

"Oh no, you're wrong there," said Bill, "He was a footballer." Poor ol' Bill, three in a row and a bonus point.

"He might have been a brilliant footballer," Ernie assured him, "In fact he could have turned professional with several big clubs. But, he could easily have turned professional as a boxer as well, he was probably the best of all of them."

"Yes," said Charlie, "He was brilliant."

Ernie was smiling, -- Bill wrong three times in one lunch break.

"I'm not so sure about boxing," Dave the digger said, "I had a mate in London who was so mad on boxing he even lied about his age.

By the time he was eighteen, he had two cauliflower ears, a completely flat nose, you could hardly understand him when he spoke, and it was lethal to go with him on a double decker bus. As soon as the conductor went ding-ding with the bell, he got up and punched the nearest person to him!" Everybody laughed.

Just as Dave finished the joke he noticed the flames leaping from Charlies sandwich, and, unlike the rest of us who'd seen it happen dozens of times, he thought he would be saving the workshop and everyone in it, so with his bare hands he swiped it right off the top of the stove -- unfortunately it shot straight into the litter bin, which meant that not only did Charlie lose his lunch yet again, but the bin caught fire! In all the pandemonium that followed, I realized that lunch break was definitely over, and back to work we went.

I suppose I have just time to tell you two more stories before the chapter runs out. One that Johnny the coal shared with us on another occasion around the stove, and a quickie from Digger Dave.

"DONKEY'S EARS APART"

Johnny remembered getting a phone call that went something like this.

" - - - LA! Is that Johnny the coal man?"

"Yes!"

"Ah! It's Mrs.Le Lachuer from Torteval."

"Yes."

"Ah! Only I wondered, me, if you could bring me some coal?"

"Where abouts is that to Mrs.Le Lachuer?"

"Ah! It's in the lane, - - by the church, - - you know, next door to Nellie Gallienne, it's Daisy Cottage."

"How much coal do you want?"

"LA! - - - better make it a ton, can you put it in the pig-sty?"

"The pig-sty?"

"It's alright - - It's alright, there's a coal bunker in there, it's to the bottom of the garden."

"Right! let me check I've got it right, you want a ton of coal, - - Daisy Cottage in a coal bunker, inside the pig-sty at the bottom of the back garden?"

"Yes,that's right, - - the money will be in Harolds trousers."

"Harolds trousers?"

"That's right, they'll be hanging up in the toilet!"

STUNNED SILENCE!

"See! there's an old outside toilet, we don't use it any more, it's to the bottom of the garden next to the pig-sty. There's a pair of Harolds trousers hanging on the nail in there, - - - the money will be in the pocket."

John said, "I went out there, backed all the way down the drive, emptied a ton of coal in the coal bunker in the pig-sty, the money was in the trousers in the toilet exactly as she had said. Two weeks later I got a phone call."

"LA! Is that Johnny the coal man?"

"Yes!"

"Ah! It's Mrs.Le Lachuer from Tortival - - - only, - - - er - - - - you've killed Harolds cat."

Now at this point it doesn't seem very likely because John had backed all the way down very carefully, and if he'd had an accident involving the cat he presumably would have seen it when coming back up the drive, so all he can think to say is :--

"Pardon?"

"You've killed Harolds cat!"

"I - - - I don't think so Mrs.Le Lachuer!"

"Yes! - - you've killed Harolds cat, he likes to sleep in the coal bunker."

Now there's silence John's end, because he has a terrible problem fighting back the laughter, with tears in his eyes, a big red face and biting his lip, all he could think to say was:--

"In the coal bunker! are you sure?"

"Oh yes," she says - - -

"Harolds just been down there with the shovel, - - - he's as flat as a pancake!!!"

* * * * * * * * * * * *

Digger Dave came into the workshop one morning grinning from ear to ear, because he'd just met a mate who used to go stealing for a living. One day he got caught, charged with a serious burglary, he got five years. Dave had just bumped into him in the street and asked him how he was getting on.

"Great!" his mate said, "You've got everything you could wish for in prison now. I even done an Open University Course while I was in there!"

Dave said, "You can't be serious?"

"Oh yes," he said, "Open University Course in Sociology - - - and I've got a P.H.D."

"What, you've got a P.H.D. in Sociology?"

"Yep!"

"What are you doing for a living now then?"

"Oh I'm still thieving, - - but now I know what makes me do it!"

CHAPTER THREE

CATCH A FALLING STAR

Since last writing about Ken 'Tiger Deano' Cataroche, I'm happy to say that up to the time of writing he is still around, I can also report that the unique singing voice he possesses has not deteriorated at all, even though in his sixty fifth year. There is of course a reason for that but least said soonest mended, Ken has now added 'Diamond' to his stage name, to give it a bit more sparkle. It was with this added extra that 'Tiger Diamond Deano' performed on Radio Guernsey. It came about in this way. During a big charity sponsor event Radio Guernsey decided that any member of their listening audience who would pledge a certain sum of money could nominate the recording of their choice. The whole of the 'Red Lion Crowd' thought it would be wonderful to send in a copy someone had made of Tiger singing. Then every second or third record that played someone would phone up from the 'Red' and ask could we have Tiger

Diamond Deano singing Wooden Heart, or could we have Tiger Diamond Deano singing Secret Love etc.

They nearly reduced the disc jockey to tears, and the person answering the studio phone began to ask searching questions like, "Why?" and "Are you sure?"

You will also have noticed that the public thoroughfares in their wisdom, put in a cycle path from the tram sheds to Richmond corner, just so that Kenny could pedal from the Red Lion to the London House in safety - - - - although using Ken's cycling and safety in the same sentence is grossly misleading.

However you will see by this latest newspaper cutting that he doesn't get much better luck when he's walking.

"CATCH A FALLING STAR."

Kenneth Cataroche was seen hanging on to a wall near the tram sheds Les Banques, and then falling into the road. When approached by a policeman all he could say was 'Tiger.' Cataroche (64) pleaded guilty in the magistrates court to lying drunk in the open air. He told the court that he was known all over the world and that he was a star. Magistrate Anthony Gillett fined Cataroche £35 . . . . I have never seen a man who loves to entertain as much as Kenny does, and I'm so glad that, by and large, the people in the different pubs he visits, join in the spirit of the occasion. There's always a clap and a cheer and usually a pint on offer too, that way everybody's happy, especially the Tiger!

Some time ago in Saumarez Park I was walking along the tar-mac roadway where I could hear the excited voices of some boisterous lads on the grassy area obscured from my view by trees and bushes, suddenly I heard a sad plaintive cry of an elderly man.

"Ahhh -- give me back my cap - eh! It was a voice, and a phrase, to make time stand still. Just then a tweed cap came streaking through the air on its way to the huge rhododendron bush, then shuffling through the trees came the owner, in full pursuit of his head-gear. It was none other than Stan the man.' A man whom I knew to be a retired policeman stood nearby keeping his eye on his two grandchildren, he looked across and was smiling at Stan's attempts to retrieve the recent flying object from the bushes, and then he said to me, "We used to do that!"

"So did we," I said, and it would appear so have every generation of youngsters since. "Poor old Stan," I said picking up a long branch with which to retrieve the cap.

"Ahhh, -- my cap! my cap!" he was saying when I reached him. I reached up and hooked it out, and no sooner had it hit the ground and he'd picked it up, put it back on his head, and rushed as quickly as his ancient feet would carry him straight back to the lads, telling them, "You're naughty boys, naughty boys, taking my cap," surely knowing full well they would tease him some more. Then off would go the cap again, after all it's been going on for forty years now.

"Poor old Stan!" I said, going back to where the retired policeman was still standing.

"Poor old Stan," he said laughing, "He loves it!"

I nodded, it was true he loved company,

and was always where the crowd was, especially the youngsters, always at all the shows. The South, The west, and the Vier Marche, the trades exhibition, the old Ideal homes exhibition, the regattas, the water carnivals, St.Georges Hall, the Odeon, the Gaumont, and more recently Beau Sejour. Always smart to go out, black blazer, grey flannel trousers and his tweed cap. Usually with his bicycle if it was daylight, though we often had his company on the picture - bus late at night. I remember it as though it were yesterday out would come the old harmonica and we'd ask him for different tunes all the way home.

Home for Stan depended on what year it was, because, he was one of seven children, he had three brothers and three sisters, each one of the families would keep Stan for a year then they would have five years break before having him again. During this time Stan worked at Maison Carre in the arcade, washing the pots and big baking trays, he worked there for many years, before transferring to Bordeaux Bakery a few years before retiring. As the families died off the remaining ones had him for longer spells, and when living with his final sister, her husband died and both she and Stan decided to go into the beautiful St Johns Hostel at Saumarez Park.

If your visiting the hostel any time, you may be sure to find Stan, carrying two lottery tickets for the next draw, which took him several hours to pick, and then he spends much of the day going from one to the other asking, "Which of these two will win the prize?" So you must pick one, and off he goes clutching them both, knowing which will be the winner, until he asks the next person and they choose the other one!

"He's a bit special is Stan," said the policeman, bringing me back to the present with a bit of a jolt.

"Yes," I sighed, "Even when we were young I never felt we were in any danger with Stan."

"My dear man," he said, calling to the grandchildren to fetch the ball back."The only danger when Stan was with the youngsters was what they might do to him!! he's a very rare breed is our Stan, one of lifes innocents, a very rare breed indeed."

Incidently on a recent visit to the hostel of St.John at Saumarez Park I not only saw Stan, but other much loved characters, such as, the now almost totally blind Jim Le Page, who loves to sit outside on one of the benches and play his accordion for the enjoyment of all who are passing by, both local and visitor alike. And also Guernseys best loved milkman, Grandes Rocques Wilf, whom you must have passed many many times, with his cap and blue tinted glasses, daily delivering his milk, pulling it along between the wayside cheer and Galaad chapel in a hand cart.

Talking of visits, I made one some time ago that I can highly recommend. I went and passed a very enjoyable hour at the Priaulx Library. On entering I asked if I could view the 'Hassall Colection.' Bernard Hassall a man of vision in the nineteen sixties realized, as indeed I did myself in the seventies, that the marvellous characters around town would not always be with us and so set about photographing as many as he could, the result was that after keeping them at home for sometime, he decided to copyright them, mount them on white card and present them to the Priaulx Library so that more people could have the enjoyment of them. It is a great collection, for a start I would estimate that there are at least two dozen photographs of Harold Selby Wake Davidson, known affectionately locally as 'Can-Can.' Even some, if my memory serves me right, in full Scottish regalia, that alone is worth the visit. Then there was the Sikh gentleman who used to sell things from door to door, wearing a turban and carrying a suitcase, Mr.Singh! Little Johnny Priaulx a tiny little man with an enormous cap, or did the cap look so big, because John was so small. One who wasn't familiar to me, but I was intrigued by her nick name, 'Two Gun' Dot Bisson, apparently she would sometimes appear wearing the belt, the holsters, and a pair of Colt 45's. Another who was familiar to me was 'Korky (Jersy Joe) Corson,' who used to own Korkies market in the former H.J.Brouard fertilizer store, opposite the bus terminus next to the Yacht Hotel. But then I turned one over that made time stand still. It was the man we kids used to call 'Reverend fag ash,' this dear old chap who presumably had to fend for himself in his twilight years, could regularly be seen going through town wearing a battered old 'trilby' carrying a shopping bag, and with egg stains and cigarette ash all down the front of his white dogs collar and black vest. Many people assumed he only dressed up as a vicar, but from what I have been able to put together, he was a very gifted and intellectual man. Listed in who's who? as Reverend G.W. Roberts, (sometimes affectionately known as Great Western Railway because of his initials), a very considerable theological mind. Whatever the whole story, I must say when I turned the photo over, it sure was good to see him again.

Finally I remember seeing in the collection a photograph of the well known motor cyclist and marathon Rock & Roller Ernie Duncombe. Ernie was the son of Charlie Duncombe whom I wrote about in 'Donkey's Ears Ago.' He was very quick indeed on a motor bike and a constant 'thorn in the flesh' to speed cop Noel Trotter. Noel was known to be a hard man but fair, and it was his unwritten rule that he would only book you if he got alongside you to flag you down. On several occasions he ended up tearing through country lanes in pursuit of a crouched over the handlebars Ernie. Easily close enough to read the number plate, but not reckless enough to pull alongside. Several days later he would pass Ernie and the motor cycle gang, and grinning from ear to ear wag a gloved finger at him to say'Next time Ernie, next time!!'

Sadly Ernie passed on some time ago, but it was good to be reminded again through the Hassal Collection. I suppose most people's ultimate photographic memory of him would be the time, all those years ago, when together with his sister Delia, they jived their way not only to marathon victory, but even into the Guinness Book of Records.

CHAPTER FOUR

THE SQUARE THAT ISN'T!!

Having grown up in Hauteville for the first ten years of my life, I have a soft spot for, and many happy memories of, Trinity Square, but lets face it, with all the good will in the world, it's not a square is it? It's a triangle. Of course in those days it wasn't beautifully paved in granite set stones with concrete troughs for bushes and shrubs as it is now. It was hard packed clay, with indentations made with the heel of someones best school shoes for the purpose of playing marbles, Ahhh! Happy days of clay dabs and steelys and Alecs. Right in the centre of this triangular 'square' was the telephone box, not some modern upright glass coffin as we have today, this was the solid, old fashioned wooden one with a proper pointed sloping roof, and when you picked up the phone you put three pennies in the box and a real person said, "Number please." You said central one two one two and got Vaudins taxis. Not like today, before you can get the thing to your ear, a robot says, "Please replace the handset and try again! Please replace the handset and try again! Please replace the handset and try again!"You scream in temper, "Ah shaddup!!" and slam it down, and as you pick it up to start again, this same aggravating robot says, "The other person has cleared. The other person has cleared. The other person has cleared"

"How can they for goodness sake? I haven't got through yet!!" That's it I'm afraid, the first signs of madness your arguing with a machine.

Fixed around the outside of the box or kiosk on three sides was a bench seat, it was on this that many of the local Trinity characters would sit. In 'Donkey's Ears Ago' I wrote of some of the people I remembered from on the square, 'Ma' Knight who ran Knights Cafe for over forty years, the two elderly spinster 'Renouf' sisters who ran the old sweet shop opposite the pump, (where the motor cycle shop is now). The dusty old toy shop opposite the Brittania Pub which has been knocked down to make space for the phone box and seats that are in that corner now. I also wrote of 'Little

John' Clarice who came twice a day, every day to fetch his water from the pump. However, I only touched on the fringes then because, right back to the days when ol' Ben Salisbury used to do his turn with the policemans helmet, there have been many many characters around there. One that springs to mind is, up to the time of writing, still around, and he's a life time Trinity man and that's big Sam Coyd. He is really Jack, but he got stuck with his big brother Sams name, after he had emigrated to Canada. Big Sam can usually be found early morning in the church doorway waiting for the paper shop to open. He usually catches me up to date with any item I may have missed from the previous days Guernsey Evening Press. Usually with a few extra caustic remarks, especially if the item is about the States!! It usually starts with "What do you think they're doing now?"

I've just thought of another Sam from the Trinity area and that was the newsagent Sam Druee, he not only had the newspaper shop at the very bottom of Victoria Road, but also the shop attached to it in lower Vauvert, the toy shop at the foot of Bouillion steps.

Now I know what you're thinking, what's all this about Ben Salisbury and the policemans helmet. Well the way my Dad used to tell it, it went like this.

Ol' Ben used to come down into the square during the evening, and bet half a dozen lads a penny each that he would knock the policemans helmet off. Then, with beer at tuppence a pint he would go into the Brittania, pass a pleasant hour or so, then come out and say, "Ready lads?" Walk up behind the policeman and knock his helmet to the floor. When the officer bent down to pick it up he would receive a prompt boot in the rear. This of course was too much, even for the most easy going 'Bobby' and Ben was swiftly marched all the way up to the Police Station. (No calling for a police van in those days). Once there, he was put inside over night, and most often let go again next morning, which was fine by him as he had'nt anywhere to sleep for the night anyway. In fact, so much was being incarcerated overnight part of the plan that sometimes he said "Ready lads" and they said, "No! it's alright Ben, don't bother with him, forget the penny."

He would say, "Not at all, not at all, I always honour a bet," and off would go the policemans helmet.

It was this same Ben who used to put a penny in the Trinity post box and look up at the church clock to see what weight he was.

One lady that everybody loved was Hilda who lived in Back Street and was permanently in a wheel chair. You would probably remember her best either by the bench seats in the corner near the telephone box, or being pushed in the wheelchair by her sisters May and Eva between Trinity Square and Cour du Parc flats.

Another couple who could be found enjoying the sun and a 'take out' cup of tea from Knights Cafe were Charlie and Maudie Pengelley. They must have chatted to hundreds in that corner over the years, yet such is the way with memory, that when I think of them it is always chatting to Ethel, another well remembered character from the area.

Yes it was a good district, a happy district. You could get your newspapers and magazines from either Druee's or Huberts. Your shoes done at Paul Le Marquand's little cobblers shop. Your meat from Belben's contree Mansell or your hair cut at Sammy's.

In a way of course, it's not without a few characters even now, as I said before big Sam is still around, and when I passed down recently Stan the Harley and Mad Max were leaning on the railings looking down into Bordage - - - Now that would be a chapter on it's own.

Both ride with the Islanders M.C. and you might well have read in the local press some years ago that Max took just one hour and thirteen minutes to eat his way through a twenty pound turkey and two dozen potatoes, thereby raising a lot of money for B.B.C.'s children in need appeal. Such is his sense of humour, that he confided in me a few days later, "No one else knows this, but I got peckish on the way home and stopped in for a bag of fish & chips!"

CHAPTER FIVE

ELVIS LE POIDEVIN LIVES

One of the regulars around the old stove at lunchtimes was the firms cleaner El. El was short for Elvis, and shows what a wicked sense of humour someone had in giving him the nickname, for as I mentioned in 'Donkey's Ears Ago' no one in the world was less like Elvis than El.

Looking back after all these years, makes me realize how much of a soft spot all the men had for El, and also the amazing assortment of descriptions they used when describing his problem. For instance Ernie would say, "Ol' El, he's a lovely bloke but he hasn't got all his chairs at home!" or "He's not a full shilling," or Let's be fair he's not dealing from a full deck."

Charlie says one day he overheard El talking to a visitor out by the gate. He thinks he'd been giving the visitor directions, when the visitor said to El, "I take it you're local." El drew himself up to his full height. "NO I AM NOT" He said most emphatically, "I'M A

GUERNSEYMAN AND PROUD OF IT!!

Can you imagine it? said Charlie, shaking his head, "I'm sure he has'nt got both paddles in the water."

The trouble with remembering the classic ones that El said is not having written them down. In the same way as young parents think they will always remember the funny things their toddler said, yet with the passing of time, sadly, we do forget.

I do remember once, when cars were being discussed around the lunchtime stove, it was a couple of weeks before Christmas. El suddenly announced, "I'll have to tax my insurance soon, I've only got three weeks to go, it runs out in June!"

No wonder Artie says, "There's a light on upstairs but nobody's home."

I was also present the day he tried to impress Ernie with what he ate.

"Every day," he said, "Without fail, for my dinner, I have potatoes except Sundays. Sundays I have chips."

His driving test by now has become a legend, part of the folklore of the firm. Apparently, the driving examiner asked El what goes in the following sequence:- Green,orange, red, red, red & orange, green, and El said, "Is it a packet of fruit gums?" The driving examiner realizing that in El's case, 'the elevator doesn't go up to the top floor,' and wishing to give him another chance said, "Well! I was thinking more of traffic lights, let me put it another way, in the sequence what comes after green?"

And El said, "I don't know I've usually gone by then!!"

There is a long established story that goes back many years before I joined as an apprentice, that the storeman saved El's life once up in the top storeroom. Standing near the open door, where the lift hoist brings up stores from way down in the yard, was El wearing, unusually for him, a pair of gum boots. Sensing by his stance that he was about to leap, the storeman called him back and after a short chat, realized that all the misunderstanding had come about because El had heard Ernie say that his brother flew 'Wellingtons' during the war. Whether there is any truth in the story I have my doubts, but either way you can see why some insist that poor ol' El is 'two sandwiches short of a picnic.

CHAPTER SIX

REMEMBER (HIC") THE BRISEIS

One of those freezing cold, rainy days you sometimes get in Autumn, which makes you fear that Winter has come early. I got myself soaking wet riding to my place of employment I euphemistically refer to as 'Stalag Ten.' My first job on such a morning was as always, to get the stove crackling and warm by lunch. After busying myself with a few small jobs around the bench, nine thirty crawled around, I closed down the bottom ventilator carefully with my foot, and got to my upturned 'snowcem' drum as the men ambled over from work benches, vacuum flasks tucked carefully under the arm.

"Well," said Artie, settling himself down in the warm, "It's my Silver Wedding Anniversary today."

This took everyone by surprise, and amidst the mumbled well dones and congratulations, he spoke again.

"Yes! October the first, nineteen thirty

seven, it was the same day the Briseis went down!

"Oh," said George quick as a flash, "Two disasters in one day eh Art!!" Everyone roared with laughter, and even Artie had to smile.

"Well bless us and save us," Ernies voice floated across, "Who'd have thought we'd live to see the day, the old Briseis eh! My, there were some shinanagins that day!" Everyone laughed again.

"Free booze for the entire west coast inhabitants," said Charlie, standing to place a cheese sandwich on the make shift toaster, "Even the kids were tiddly."

I couldn't resist finding out more. "Why? what happened?" I asked.

"What happened," said Artie, who would normally have dozed off in the warm by now, but it was his wedding day under discussion. "What happened? this ship the three thousand ton French steamer Briseis hit the grunes reef and sank. Her whole cargoe broke loose and was floating off the west coast. People were wading into the sea to pull the barrels ashore."

"What barrels?" I inquired.

"The wine barrels, the wine barrels," said Ernie impatiently, "That's what she was carrying, thousands of gallons of Algerian red wine."

"Were all the crew lost at sea?" I asked.

"No - No," said Ernie, "None of 'em were lost, they manned two fair sized life boats and rowed clear of the wreck."

"That's right," Bill came into the discussion, "And they came across the Bewey brothers from the Vale, and followed them into Grand Havre, that's where they came ashore, Grand Havre!"

Just then there was a panic in our midst, and the sound of gale force winds as Charlie tried to blow out his cheese cinder.

"That's Nothin', that's nothin'," he said to no one in particular, "We'd 'ave been glad of this in the occupation, and as he'd done on so many previous occasions he sank his teeth into the charcoal mass, as he chewed some of the black stuck to one of his teeth making it appear that he had gaps what Georgie used to call football pools teeth, one home and one away.

Five hundred barrels found their way back

HAROLD 'CAN-CAN' DAVIDSON

BILLY ROSWELL

STEVE PICQUET

JERBOURG NEWSBOY DERECK

FRED 'THE GAS' PAGE

REGGIE LAMB

to the States bond store. They were offering a pound a barrel reward for them. I was just thinking that's not much when Artie came back in again.

"Any fisherman who found nine or ten of those got himself a couple of weeks wages like that."

"He might well have done," said Bill, "But he would have earned his money, they were bloney heavy those wine barrels, they held 120 gallons."

"Bless us and save us," said Ernie, "120 gallons, that's what they call a hogshead isn't it?"

"I don't know," said Bill, "But you wouldn't want it on your foot, that's for sure!!"

"There was a lot more than five hundred on board," said Charlie, having managed to consume his lightly grilled cheese delicacy, "A lot more!! My mate was a policeman at the time and he said that you've never seen anything like the west coast during that time. By the time he'd rode out to the Vazon coast from town by bicycle there were men, normally very respectable men, with their caps on sideways, staggering and pointing in the general direction of Pleinmont, and calling out to him, ISH FURDER ALONG, ISH FURDER DAT WAY, and then they'd fall over, men, women and children were everywhere carrying anything that would hold liquid, from galvanized baths to hot water bottles.

I asked him if his instructions were to arrest anyone carrying bottles or rolling barrels along. He said, "No, the police chief, (Oh what was his name).

"Lamy," said Bill.

"No, No," Charlie said, "It was before Lamy." - - - "Sculpher that was him.

My mate said his chief, 'Sculpher' was much too practical for that, their only instruction was, all drunk bodies found on the beach must be dragged above the high water mark! Everyone laughed at that.

"There was smaller barrels as well," commented Artie, still awake! "I remember some more normal size ones, in fact I know what happened to one of them"

"Oh yes," said Charlie, "They were the spirit barrels there was gin in some of them, and a very fiery raw North African Brandy. I don't know what it tasted like, but they reckon your car would have run for a hundred miles on one bottle." Again there was laughter it was obviously potent stuff.

"Go on then Art," Charlie urged gently, "What happened to one of them?"

"Well!"Art began, "This bloke I know of, rolled a barrel of gin or whatever along the coast road to his bungalow. He knew it was no good hiding it in the shed, he figured that would be the first place anyone would look, his bungalow was cream, and his front door, windows, and the gutters and downpipes were in a sort of jade green. He had a rain-water barrel on the front left hand side, painted cream, and the steel bands in jade green. So what he did was, he stood the barrel up on end, painted it cream and green to match the other one, painted a spare length of downpipe in the appropriate green and jammed it between the top of the barrel and the gutter. The two barrels stood one each end of the front of his bungalow for ages till everything had blown over. Then he tapped it, and filled his bottles." Everyone smiled and nodded approvingly at this. With stories like this it made one wish Artie would stay awake more often.

"Fifty six gallons," quoted Charlie right out of the blue.

The rest looked from one to the other as if they'd somehow missed a sentence.

"The smaller ones, that's what they held, fifty six gallons."

"Oh," said someone.

In the ensuing silence that followed I wondered if there was such a thing as half-a-hogshead.

"Of course you know," announced Ernie breaking the silence, "It's what Compton Mckenzie based his best selling book -- 'Whisky Galore' on."

"Book," said Bill, "I thought it was a film."

"Yes - yes," Ernie said, "It is a film, but the film is based on the book, and the book is based on the sinking of the Briseis."

"Where'd you get that from?" said Bill, in his usual argumentative way, "Whisky Galore is set in Scotland."

"Yes!" a little bit of exasperation creeping into Ernies voice. "I know it's set in a little Island off the coast of Scotland, but, Compton M^c^kenzie was living on Jethou when it went down and that's what gave him the idea."

"Ah well," said Bill starting to rise, "You'd know more about these things than me, you being a townie!"

Then he said those words so painful to me, "I suppose we'll have to." Lunch was over - - - the best bit of the day and it was finished.

* Footnote:- The first man on the scene at the sinking of the Briseis was Mr.James Le Page of Lilyvale Castel. The motor vessels which finally towed the life boats into Grand Havre, belonged to Mr.J.Jehan, Mr.E.Girard and Mr.T.Carre as well as the Bewey's.

CHAPTER SEVEN

'MARJORIE' AND THE MUSINGS OF MEMORY

I recently came across a book published in 1963 and written by E.V.Coltman called :- 'Birds of the Storm.' It was a biography of Marjorie Ozanne and her bird hospital. It took my mind back again to the lunchtime stories around the stove. The subject on the bygone day in question was the contribution of some of our local ladies to the community, you know the sort of thing I mean. For example, if we were talking today it would be someone like Sister Lincoln, or the late deputy Valerie Renouf. But in those days, names like Lady Ozanne came up. Lady Ozanne founded the first Maternity hospital, another was Mabel Poat a lady constantly on the go, involved in all sorts of charitable causes, always trying to help others! Other names included, Emma Ferbrache and Matron Bones, then inevitably Marjorie Ozanne and her bird hospital. This is how the dust jacket notes describe her:-

BIRDS OF THE STORM

The story of Marjorie Ozanne's bird hospital on Guernsey really began in 1940 when the Nazis occupied the Island. Many of those who escaped to the mainland left behind their pet birds, which Marjorie rescued and sheltered in her own home. Aided by her friend Nell, she carried on her own secret "war" with the Nazis to save them from destruction and feed and protect those injured and helpless.

Against a fear-laden background she dedicated herself to rescuing and protecting the birds, half-starving herself and bartering clothes and shoes in order to provide them with food. Her concern was such that eventually even the Germans helped her, including the dignified, jackbooted Dr.Ortmann. The storm of war passed, but the winds and seas continued to batter Guernsey and leave bird-victims in their wake. Marjories hospital also continued and today she is famous throughout Europe for her ornithological knowledge and experience in the treatment of sick birds; it is a fame well justified: her hospital cares for hundreds of birds every year, ranging from toucans and seagulls to puffins and cormorants. Some have been injured and marooned on cliff faces and rocks, others have become oil-clogged. In the majority of cases it is a matter of life and death. Her patients overflow into her home, taking over the bedroom and bathroom, but her biggest headache are those who don't wish to leave her.

This is essentially a "bird" book, but it is also a human story, providing a graphic example of how the Samaritan instinct can exist and persist against the most adverse circumstances.

There is no doubt about the fact that Marjorie, was one hundred percent, Guernsey. A real local character, I think the story I like best is one Ernie told us all those years ago, and I notice is reiterated in the book. He said, not long after the Germans had landed an order was given that every pigeon on the Island was to be killed. This to prevent messages getting to England. Marjorie who had just spent months bringing one back from the throes of death, was in no-way going to kill it, so she got hold of some drummer dye, boiled it, and then let it cool down. When no one else was around she painstakingly painted every individual feather black. This she touched up every six months and the pigeon happily saw the war out as a crow. I love this story because I think there is something in the Guernsey spirit that likes to put one over on authority, any authority! Like the man with the cream and jade green barrel, or more recently the man on the outskirts of St.Peter Port who asked the I.D.C. for permission to knock down the tiny wall in his front garden to enable him to bring his car into his garden, instead of outside blocking a busy major road. They refused, so he dismantled the little wall, and built it again identically on a steel frame with a pair of heavy duty hinges one end and a single wheel on the garden-side at the other end. Now whilst he is at work all day his wall remains as always but when he arrives home at night he swings open his wall, drives in, out of everyones way and then closes the wall again.

I suppose we like to put one over on authority like this, because of a strange quirk in nature, whereby as soon as anyone is given any kind of authority the power goes straight to their head. Like the story of the poor Railway Signalman in England who wanted to be made up to Chief Signalman just so he could earn an extra fiver a week, down came a power crazed committee to test him out to see if he would qualify as a Chief Signalman. There was no way they were going to make it easy for this poor chap.

"Now," said the first one, "What would you do if you found that you had a downtrain and an uptrain coming towards your signal box on the same line?"

"Well," said the signal man, "I would quickly press this button over here on the panel and that would switch the uptrain onto another track."

"Ah," said another, trying to be awkward, "What if when you pressed it, it didn't work?"

"Well then," he said, "I would quickly press this other button over here and that would switch the down train onto a different track."

"Ah!" said another, "Supposing when you press it that didn't work either?"

"Well then," he said, holding his patience well, "Quick as a flash I would tear five hundred yards up the track and pull the manual lever over and thereby put the downtrain on to the other track."

"AHH," said the first one again, "What if when you got there, the lever , because of rust and corrosion wouldn't budge?"

"Well then," he said in desperation, "Fast as I could, I would run back to the signal box, up the steps, and press the Emergency button up in the top corner there! That puts every signal in the area at stop!!"

"AHHH!" said yet another, "What if when you ran back to the signal box, it was on fire, and you couldn't get in to the emergency button?"

"Well then," said our intrepid hero, "With

all the strength I had left I would race five hundred yards down the track, to the bungalow down there and call Harry!"

"Why," said the first one again, "Would you do that?"

"Because," said the signal man, "Harry is my mate, and he's never seen a train crash!!"

* * * * * * * * * * *

Memory is a subject I find fascinating. I once watched a documentary programme on television about a man who had previously worked for the B.B.C. and had suffered total memory loss, he went about all day saying to everyone; The most amazing thing is, I have just woken up. Just this minute woken up and I can't remember a thing. It nearly drove one mad to hear him time and time again, but what struck me even more was the absolute annihilation of his quality of life, even though the rest of his health was good, his quality of life seemed to me destroyed. Because music was so very important to him, friends organized for him to do, what under normal circumstances would have been the highlight of his life, they took him to conduct the Halle Orchestra, this they also video recorded. Later at home when they played it back with him they said, "Surely you must remember doing this."

He said, "I can see that I did, and I can well imagine that I would have loved it, but sadly, the thing is, that I have just this minute woken up and I can't remember a thing." - - - - Boy that is some memory loss!

The dictionary describes memory as:- exemption from oblivion, this must be worthwhile surely, in case it is ever later of any value, after all each of us have used memories, in forming opinions, colouring our outlook, and coming to decisions, thereby partially at least developing our personality. I wonder if in this life at least, it might be said to a limited degree:- "I am what I remember!" Happily our future is not tied into this, for to receive the gift of Eternal Life, which after all is the point of us being here. Travelling through this rapidly passing three score years and ten, the whole work has been accomplished on our behalf, by someone else. To receive Him is to receive the gift, and the security of this is not in retaining the memory of the transaction, but rather we can say with the Apostle Paul:-

"I know in whom I have believed, and am persuaded that 'HE' is able to keep that which I've committed unto 'HIM' against that day."

Another fascinating thing about memory is the speed involved, faster surely than any computer, a name, a smell anything can send it flashing back ten years, twenty, thirty. Let me give an example. If I write the words to John Longmire's lovely 'Song of Welcome' there should be a whole generation, who can immediately remember the tune that goes with it:-

Sing sweetest music on this festal day.
Bring flowers to greet them let the streets be gay,
gay with the songbird singing in the air
when beauty comes we welcome her with music everywhere.

Back comes the memory, not only the tune but all the rehearsals at school, and then the big day, the Royal visit at Cambridge Park. Thinking back I remember not only the rehearsals but also the lady who had the unenviable task of teaching it to us. Miss Mabel Le Pelley was the music teacher at St.Andrews school, and just recently, I had the joy of spending an evening of conversation with her, in this her ninety second year. Up 'till only just recently she had been swimming all the year round in the great tradition of Guernsey year-round swimmers such as Bill Green and the late Ralph Palmer. It seemed strange, whilst listening to her converse so articulately on a wide range of subjects, that many of her earliest pupils, from St.Peters school, her first and only other school, had died of old age.

She began her teaching career at St.Pierre du Bois school under the headship of Walter Brehaut a very able Christian man who I mentioned in 'Donkey's Ears Ago.' There is a story about Walter Brehaut that I like very much, it was to do with a boy at the school who drove some of the teachers almost to despair because he never seemed to grasp anything they were telling him, and seemed to have very little knowledge of anything at all. In desperation he was called to the head-masters office. After spending some time talking, Mr.Brehaut said, look son is there anything at all you are interested in, and he said:

"Yes sir, motor cars."

Well said Walter get some paper and go away and write everything you know about motor cars. Not long after, back came the boy they all feared knew nothing at all. He had filled both sides of 4 fullscap sheets on the technical workings and components of the internal combustion engine and other car related material. The boy grew up to be the Island agent for Wolsey and Riley cars and owner of the large garage business at Le Merriennes, you've guessed it 'Le Lachuer's.

As well as St.Andrews school I went to three others. In one such school the teacher asked the question, "Who knocked down the walls of Jericho, after a pause Billy Falla put his hand up and said;

"Please Miss it wasn't me."

The teacher outraged by the ignorance

shown in the answer given, and the low standard in general, went to the head master to complain.

She said, I just asked the class who knocked down the walls of Jericho, and Billy Falla said, please Miss it wasn't me. The headmaster thought about this a moment and then said, "Well! I have known the Falla family for many many years, and if little Billy said it wasn't him, then it wasn't him" This left her flabbergasted, so that night from her home she wrote a letter of complaint to the States Education Council, which went as follows:-

This morning I asked my class the question who knocked down the walls of Jericho and Billy Falla said; 'Please Miss it wasn't me!' I complained to the headmaster who informed me that he had known the Falla family for many many years and if Billy said it wasn't him then it wasn't him.

Some weeks later she received a reply from the States Education Council, saying we have given careful consideration to your letter and have decided that to avoid any further bad feeling, if you would go ahead and get the wall repaired we will pay the bill!!

I'll never forget the young chap in my class who came from one of the poorer districts, he got back to school late from dinner, . . . The teacher asked him, "What time do you call this?" and he said;

"I'm sorry I'm late Sir, but mum's been making home made blackberry jam, and she sent me up the cemetary to find some jars!!"

Finally I must tell you about my Dad's school days, as his interest and love of local characters and their stories, is to a large degree the reason I have become so interested myself. He said, "I was victimised by the teachers at school, they used to accuse me of cheating just because I happened to sit next to the cleverest boy in the class. I ask you, is that fair? One day the teacher called me to the front, he said; For question one John Brehaut has got Paris, and you've got Paris. For question two John Brehaut has got London, and you've got London. For question three John Brehaut has got, I do not know the answer to this question, and you've got; Neither do I!!

CHAPTER EIGHT

REMOVALS

Watching the film Buster, about the great train robber Buster Edwards, I spied in the background, lending period authenticity to the scene, a vehicle that was absolutely part of the local scene. The Ogier Bros. Bedford 'O' Series Pantechnicon yet another part of Island life, part of growing up. One of my favourite stories about the brothers, who were not really very big in stature, but very stout of heart, is the story about the delivery of a very heavy type of settee to the weight lifting club. When it was up the steps in Bordage, the power lifters and musclemen seeing the lorry arrive came down several flights of narrow stairs, offering to carry it up to the top floor club. Someone who witnessed it said, once the 'big fellers' got the thing into the narrow staircase it was bedlam. Some were pushing when they should have been lifting, some were twisting when it should have been held straight. One was very red in the face and with moist eyes as he tried to extricate his hand from between the full weight of the sofa and the wall, and there was a very real danger of the one with the purple face who was completely jammed against the bannisters crashing through the wooden structure and down onto the staircase below. It was into this mayhem that the brothers offered to try it a different way, then the three of them quietly manoeuvred it up the three flights and into the club amidst the claps and cheers of the musclemen. I suppose it's true there's no substitute for experience. Anyway they got a good tip from those who realized it wasn't as easy as it looked.

Removals is a subject I like because it abounds with stories especially once you're amongst the long distance and international boys.

I worked on it myself for a while and there is a great spirit of comradeship not only between drivers and porters but between removal men from rival firms. It is with the meeting of these, that the stories and anecdotes flow.

Unfortunately these can never be transferred

to print in the rich brogue of the district it originated in. One I remember clearly was told us by a pair of Scots movers about a mate who was doing a delivery to the Isle of Man. He phoned his manager and said, "Huloo boss, I missed the ferry!!"

"Oh no," said the manager, "This is terrible the people are already at the house waiting, whatever you do make sure you're on the next one."

Scottie replied, "I can't do that boss, I missed the ferry!!" Then there was a short pause, "It's in the water!!!"

Whilst on the subject of breaking the news gently they told of another driver, not on their firm this time, who had phoned his boss to say that he had broken his lorry's mirror.

"Well," said his boss, "You'd better go and measure it so that I can order its replacement"

"I'm afraid I can't do that," said the driver, "The lorry's laying on it!!"

As part of the training for this job I was sent to a British government transport and removals packing course in an ex U.S. air force base in a place called High Ercol near Shrewsbury. There we learnt how to pack properly, how to dismantle grand father clocks for transporting, and handling barometers without losing the quick silver. One very important thing they taught us was how to remove a sash window and then replace it. It was this that played an important part in a job I went on with Eric. We had to bring a large wardrobe down from a flat above a showroom, the staircase was too narrow, and Eric said, "Well didn't they teach you to remove a sash window at High Ercol."

I said, "Yes they did Eric, but in lowering it down the front of the building we'll break the window."

"Ah," he said tapping his nose, "They didn't teach you everything there, I've got a few tricks up my sleeve as well, you know!"

So I set about removing the window. Eric went down and got several of what we called 'ties,' they are 2 inch wide upholstery webbing bands, cut into different lengths used for tying in all the load securely. We tied on sufficient lengths to lower it all the way down to the road, then came Erics piece de resistance. He tied another length on one of the wardrobes front legs and threw the length down into the road, then went down himself, and whilst I gently lowered it from the window sill, he, using the other length of 'tie' kept it away from first the wall and then the large showroom window. He had a grin like the proverbial Cheshire cat, when it reached the ground safely. Leaving it standing there he then went into the lorry to make room for it, and I had just begun to replace the window when there was an almighty crash! The wardrobe which had been standing in the sloping gutter fell straight through the showroom window. Laugh?? I nearly passed my fags around!!

On all removal firms there is at least one man who will specialize in dropping hints for a cup of tea. We had Nobby, he was wonderful, he always managed it without anyone being offended. I wondered what on earth he was on about the first time I heard him shout, "Is that you whistling Eric?" Eric looked across at me and laughed.

"No Nobby it wasn't me whistling."

"Ah!" shouted back Nobby, "It must be the

kettle then!!"

Another day he had his newspaper out, as though he was doing a crossword puzzle. He kept asking, "Four across, plastic stems for golf balls to sit on." Nobody answered and one of the boys said, "It's too hard for me Nobby." The lady of the house couldn't resist any more and said, "Is it tees Nobby?" and he said, "That's very kind of you, all with milk and sugar please!"

I saw him do a routine once even I didn't know what he was going on about. He had found the tray, and he said to the lady, "My! but this is a lovely tray you've got here."

She said, "Oh, do you like it?"

"Like it?" he said, "I love it, it's walnut isn't it?"

"Yes, actually I believe it is!"

"Lovely," said Nobby again, "And this is Salisbury Cathedral if I'm not mistaken."

"Yes, that's right," said the lady, bewildered by Nobby's enthusiasm.

"Salisbury Cathedral, in walnut veneer. You know there's only one thing that could improve a tray of this caliber."

"And what's that?" she enquired.

"Four mugs of steaming hot tea all with milk and sugar."

The lady laughed heartily and put the kettle on.

You never really know what will crop up next in removals. Ivan was doing a move for an elderly lady one time when half way through the morning she asked, "Would you be willing to take my sister with you when you go?"

Ivan was at great pains to explain that he wasn't insured to carry passengers, when she hurriedly explained, No-No, she's not a passenger, she's in this urn on the mantel-piece, - - - Only I didn't know if someone might be offended - - - - I would tape up the lid of course.

Ivan was so pleased thats all she meant, he said, "That's okay, I'll see to it, I'll see to it," and took the urn from the mantelpiece. She went out the door and he accidently dropped it on the carpet. The lid came off and ash powder was all over the place. He quickly scooped back as much as he could, then to make sure she wasn't upset, he cleared the rest up with the vacuum cleaner.

He said to me some time later, "That poor old soul, to this day she doesn't know that half her sister is in the urn, and the other half is in her hoover!!"

Long distance runs were good fun, if you had a good mate. 'Big Chris' and I pulled into the beautiful little Yorkshire country town of Holmsfirth, where 'The Last of the Summer Wine' T.V. programmes are made. This would have been around midnight, fortunately we saw an arrow sign which said Coach Park. Sure enough as we manoeuvred the big Pantechnicon down the roadway we saw in the headlights a large tar-mac area. We parked up, drew around the windscreen and side window curtains and then began the amazing ritual of getting undressed. Balancing on one leg on spring seats, bed is one of two narrow parcel shelf arrangements placed one above the other behind the seats. So difficult is going to bed and getting up in the relatively small cab that it is often easier to do so just outside the door of the lorry.

"DONKEY'S EARS APART"

We had a good nights sleep, the big fella being the first awake in the morning, drew aside the curtains to check what kind of a day it was, and I woke up to the words, "For goodness sake don't leap out in your undies, we're in the school playground!"

Imagine that! Probably the only place in the whole country, where half the school playground doubled up as a seasonal Coach Park.

Sadly not all jobs are fun in removals. Some of the saddest are what are termed 'Split ups,' where couples who have meant so much to each other previously, are reduced to fighting over every item, every scrap of furniture 'till in the end the police have to be called in to adjudicate, right down to who gets custody of the teapot.

Another thing most people would not think of, is double handling, this sometimes happens on Ro-Ro crossings and international moves. It involves handling a whole house of furniture etc. four times. This comes about when you load the whole move from the old house, then you handle the whole move again taking it out in the customs shed. Then immediately after, when they realize you're not part of a Columbian drugs cartel, but just ordinary blokes trying to earn a weeks wages, you put it all back again, sometimes questioning how it ever went in the first time without these pieces left over. And then finally the fourth time unloading at the new house.

One good thing about continental moves is you get to meet people of other nations in their own environment, as Mick did one beautiful summer evening passing through a tiny French village, when with a horrible grating sound he stuck the huge pantechnicon under a railway bridge. It seemed as though the whole village came out to enjoy the show. Finally one older man stepped forward with the hand of friendship outstretched and a --- Parlez-Vous Francais Monsieur? on his lips. Mick who is struggling with English never mind French, said 'No.' So very carefully in his best broken English, the man began by way of conversation opener.

"Yoo 'ave stook your Camion under zer bridge?"

So Mick knowing the lorry was stuck fast, and would go neither forwards nor backwards, and feeling a fool anyway decided to be silly. He shook his head, "No!" he said, "I was delivering this bridge, when your road narrowed and it has jammed across the road."

Amazingly the man understood him, translated what he said, and all the village broke into laughter -- some even clapped. With that, the village mechanic moved in with a few gestures, and started letting two thirds of the air out of each tyre. Mick managed then to extricate the truck amidst more joyful clapping, and the mechanic led the way a couple of hundred yards to his garage which he opened up, got the air compressor going, and not long afterwards Mick was, -- 'Back on the road again!'

Because of the unexpected happenings like low bridges and dictatorial Customs men you can never work out the estimated time of arrival on continental runs. If you are a whole day late, there might well be ructions, if a whole day early you have to find something to do to kill the time.

"DONKEY'S EARS APART"

This happened to Ian and Chris-the-chef. On arriving down on the sunny south coast of Spain a day early, they decided to park up, and take a swim. On the way to the sandy beach they passed a little Spanish Bar and Ian suggested a quick drink. Chris said he would try one of Ian's usual concoctions, Ian is a Bacardi and coke man, so that is how Chris came to try his first Bacardi and coke, and he liked it. Infact he liked it a lot, not to put too fine a point on it he liked all fifteen of them, and then they continued to the beach. Ian managed to get into his bathers (swimming trunks to non-locals) quite painlessly, and Chris had got as far as wrapping the towel around him and removing his clothes. He had one leg in his bathers and in attempting to put his other one in, he hooked his foot in the waist band, naturally he lost his balance. Now! common sense tells you if you lose your balance, half in, and half out, of your bathers, to fall down in the soft sand with the least amount of fuss would be favourite. Not so fifteen bacardis, they tell you it is undignified to fall over when just a few hops will regain your balance. Unfortunately as each hop put him at a more and more acute angle to the sand the hopping took on panic proportions. By half way across this crowded beach the dignity and the towel had gone. Mothers rushed to shield the eyes of their offspring as this manic monoped careered his uncharted course across their picnic lunches only to eventually sprawl in a big heap in the soft sand which he could have done in the first place.

No wonder the Spanish have that special expression -- 'Crazee Engleesh!!!'

Whilst on a run to that tiny tax haven in the Pyrenees Andorra we became victims of yet another Spanish expression Manana. Technically it means tomorrow, but over all the picture is why do to-day what can be put off 'till tomorrow, and even when tomorrow comes, well there's no hurry.

We arrived in the mountains of Andorra only to find that the house was being built (or rather wasn't) by Spanish builders, which meant that not only wasn't the house finished but they weren't even there to lend a hand. The Spanish use a system of scaffolding which consists of rickety planks of wood nailed to even more rickety wooden poles, and leaning haphazardly against this lethal jumble of lollipop sticks was an even more lethal 'health and safety,' ignoring home made ladder. Up this we had to clamber and crawl with such things as sideboards, wardrobes and three seater settees on our backs. I still have the photo, of us, with the lady of the house who had also only just arrived at Maison de la missing staircase, and risking life and limb had climbed out of a window to help at the top of the ladder.

ERNIE & DELIA DUNCOMBE

JACK 'BIG SAM' COYD

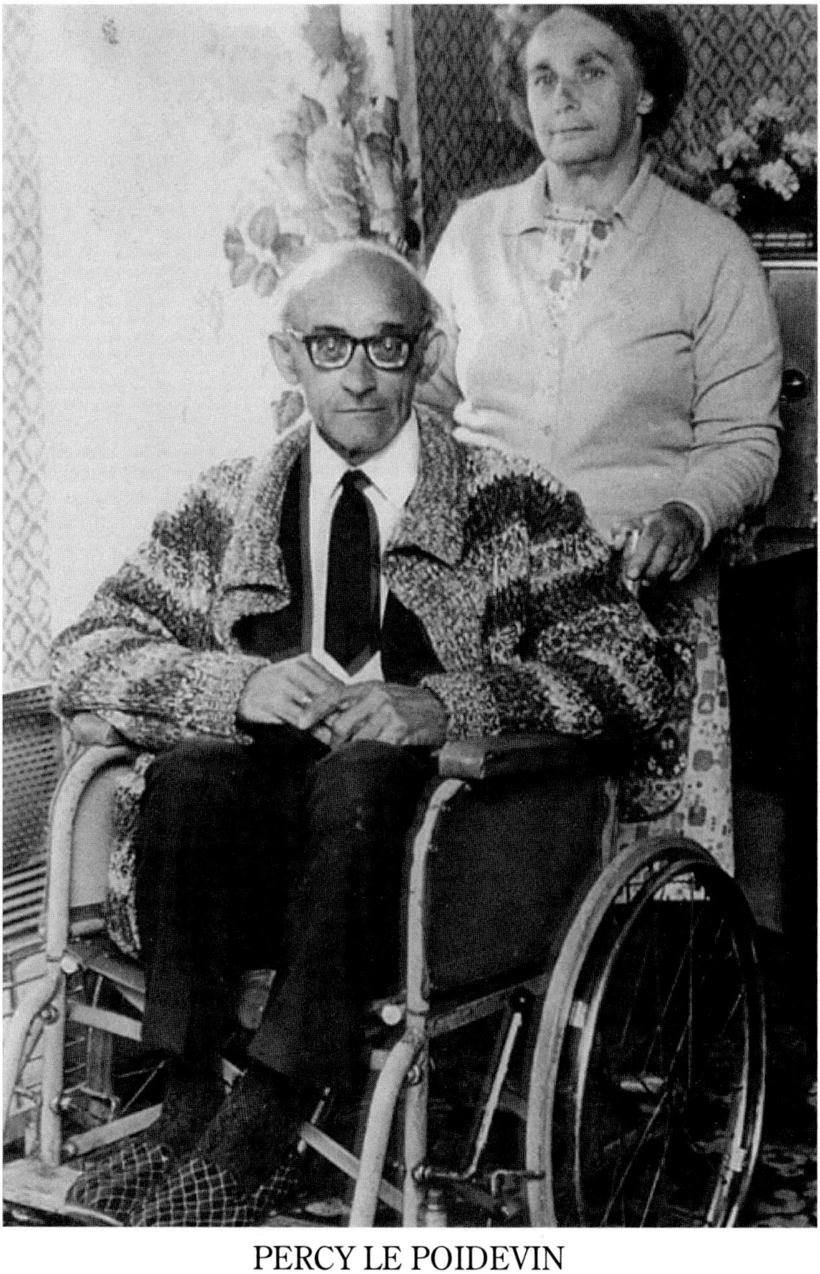

PERCY LE POIDEVIN

ROY FINCH

HERBIE RENOUF

OGIER BROTHERS

FRED RUFF

LEN BRACHE & HAROLD GUILLOU

DE BOURGONNIERE BROS.

BARRY JONES

CHAPTER NINE

FORT GEORGE

Having grown up in Hauteville as I mentioned previously, I also have happy memories of Fort George. It was a vast area stretching from the Cows Horn (Clarence Battery) to Morley Corner and belonged to the British Government. Although by the time we came along, the Sherwood Foresters and all other regiments had long gone. Much remained as it was. Firstly there was the picturesque guard room just inside the main arch gate. I remember the clock on the tower always said twenty five past five, which some people thought was of no use at all, and others thought at least like that, twice a day it was right. The soldiers living accommodation were known as lower lines, officers lines and princes lines, I still remember some of the families living there.

The Lambs, the Rolls, the Audoires, the Murphy's and the Roberts families were down on what is now part of the cliff walk from the 'cows horn' to Fermain which was known then as lower lines.

Officers lines had, the Canns, the Gibsons, and the Grieves families, this line corresponded roughly with the two houses called Edgewarebury and White Heron which replaced them. Two families on the higher up princes lines were Bretels and the Hattons. (You never forget your paper round). Many of these families were re-housed in a nice little estate called 'Couture Close,' near St.Peter Port school.

By the way, the reason the clock stopped at twenty five past five was that, on the 4th. June, 1944 when the fort was in the hands of the Germans the R.A.F. came over and attacked it with rocket and gunfire, that 'euchred' the clock.

When Rush & Tomkins started building there they took on a well known local character called 'Accident Barry,' so called because everything the foreman gave him to do, something always came off in his hand. One day the foreman, who was often in utter despair as to what he could give him to do, found the perfect job, he said Barry -- go up to the big house by the Citadel and rip out all the wood, the doors, the windows, the cupboards, the skirting boards, the picture rails, the bannisters, everything made of wood. Throw it all outside in a heap. Barry was ecstatic, being given a job and trusted on his own, he said;

"Right skip! what will I do with the heap of wood after that?"

"Don't worry about the heap," said the foreman, "We'll have a bonfire at a later date, but that's not your problem."

Barry was so keen he was running, and the foreman was smiling like the cat who had just found the cream, having found Barry the perfect job breaking things.

Barry had not long started the job when one of the site workers asked him what he was doing. Barry explained that he was ripping out all the wood and heaping it outside.

"What are they going to do with the wood when you have finished?" asked the worker.

"Have a bonfire," said Barry.

"What are they doing with the house after that?" he asked.

"Knocking it down," said Barry again.

"Barry - Barry, use your loaf," he exclaimed excitedly, "If they're only going to burn the wood, and they're knocking the place down anyway, -- Save yourself all that work and burn it in there!"

Barry thought that was positively brilliant so instead of checking with the foreman first, he went straight to the diesel store and got a large can of diesel. He then proceeded to pour it all over the ground floor, then threw on a match. Up unto the next floor and poured it all over, threw on a match, and up to the top floor. It was whilst he was busy pouring what remained of the diesel on that floor that he noticed the flames leaping up the staircase. Eye witness reports say that the bell of the fire engine on its way, could be heard whilst it was still as far away as Trinity Square, and that, above the screams and shouts coming from the top floor window.

The brigade were praised and congratulated by all except the foreman, who thought all things considered, they should have left him there, especially as he had the thankless task of finding Barry yet another job to muck up all over again tomorrow!

I would find it difficult to believe a story like this myself were it not for one of the stories Georgie told us one day around the stove at the Stalag. He and Barry went to the same school and after school they both used to go and help a farmer with the many jobs on the farm.

One day, Georgie said, when we were in the top meadow the farmer said to Barry, go down into the farmyard, the horse and cart are already harnessed up, bring them out of the yard, up the back lane and into the meadow through the top gate. Barry ran off all excitedly and we waited. After quite a while the farmer was getting a bit aggravated, "Where's that nipper now," and "It doesn't take all this time just to - - - - ." He stopped as he saw Barry running up the field towards us, his face all red and tears streaming down his face:

"The - the - there's be - be - been a terrible accident."

"I'll give you accident," said the farmer, starting to run towards the farm. Purple in the face, we were running with him. Barry still with tears in his eyes, the sight that met our gaze I'll never forget if I live to be a hundred. I had to bite my lip, I was fighting back the laughter. - - - - See! what Barry had done was, instead of getting on the cart in the normal way, he decided to ride the horse. Once he was on the horse, then the steep slope up from the bottom meadow looked a much better proposition than going all around the lane, then in through the top gate. After all, there was room! Yes! said Georgie grinning, there was room for the horse, but as he climbed higher and higher up the slope, the slope got narrower and narrower, the danger means nothing to Barry as it's all happening behind him. Eventually right near the top of the slope the wheel slipped over the edge, and the whole caboodle turned turtle, throwing Barry clear. - - - - - - By the time we got there the cart is upside down in the field and the poor ol' horse is still between the shafts with his four legs sticking straight up in the air!! The men around the stove roared with laughter, as Georgie continued. "You should 'ave heard what the farmer was calling Barry while he was cutting up a fortunes worth of leather harness, to save the poor beasts life. Even from such an early age you can see why they called him accident Barry."

To continue our journey through the fort, up at the top end near Barry's three storied house, up in the area where the radio mast and workshop is now, I remember the saints football pitch and the old wooden 'changing room' hut with a verandah on the front. To get a fix on it now, you would have to come along the fort road, just past the radio mast and workshop there is a clump of very old and large pine trees. The hut was directly in line with the pines, and the football pitch stretched from there down to three quarters of the length of the long grass lawn. Then there was from the main road a gateway to a rough track which ran up the middle with the pitch on one side and the group of nissen huts on the other. Different local families lived in this mini village of, half round, corrugated constructions.

One of these were Charlie and Maudie Pengelly and their family. This was in the nineteen fifties before they were Trinity Square people, back in the days when people used to talk about the 'daylight boat.' The days when Liptons used to sell loose biscuits from glass topped biscuit tins this side of the counter, and for a few pence you could buy a bag of 'brokes.' When five o'clock on Saturday evening you could get, for a shilling, a bag of 'stalies' from Warry's in the Bouet, perfectly good cakes that would not have lasted 'till Monday, otherwise, No-problem! The days when a wagon wheel looked like it had come off a wagon, not like a chocolate covered polo.

Anyway the Nissen huts brought us eventually to the end of the Fort George property and out to Morley Chapel, (now a youth hostel). Built in 1863 as a Wesleyan Methodist Chapel, the foundation stone was laid by the Reverend Morley Punshon, so you can see it must have been originally, Morley's Chapel. It was built when the congregation consisting of both locals and soldiers from Fort George outgrew their first chapel which was the building opposite the Rue de Putron, that we have always known as Sam's Garage.

"DONKEY'S EARS APART"

I was never really of the 'Fort George for workers homes' persuasion. I feel the houses and the layout are delightful, and with hindsight feel, the only serious error someone made was knocking down the guardhouse. With just a coat of paint and the clock repaired it would have given a certain Military pomp and presence to the area of the main gate, the entrance to the whole complex.

CHAPTER TEN

FERRIES AND HEROES

It was snowing outside, now that's pretty unusual in Guernsey. It was blowing a gale aswell, and that's not!! It was so cold that the men had actually congratulated me on getting the stove . . . 'red hot' in time for lunch. We were all seated around in the normal way, me on my drum, Charlie was rigging up a cheese sandwich for cremation.

When I see Charlies sandwiches I always think of a mate who worked for years with a man who every day at lunch opened up his package of sandwiches, peeped inside one of them, and said, "Bloney cheese again she knows I don't like cheese!" and then threw them in the bin. He said, this went on day in and day out for ages. Then one day he picked up his package of sandwiches, he said, "Bloney cheese again," and threw them in the bin.

My mate said, "You've thrown them away without even checking first."

The bloke said, "No need to check 'em to

know they're cheese today. She's ill, I had to make 'em myself."

So we were all seated around the pot bellied stove when, little Artie-the-dormouse said, to no one in particular, "How many Herm ferry names can you remember ?"

"Well bless us and save us," said Ernie, "Dearie me today next week, who'd 'ave thought we'd live to see the day, Herm Ferries eh! the old Herm Ferries," his voice finally trailed away, without naming one.

"I can remember the Bounty and the Lady June," I said getting the ball rolling.

"The Maywood and the Capwood," said Georgie.

"The Alouette and the Silouette," said Charlie dipping something into his flask cup to extinguish the flames.

"The Typhoon and the Harpoon," said Stan. I remembered another one , Highland Laddie, Arrowhead," said Stan again.

"Nobody's said -- Isle of Herm or the White Heather," said Artie, finally getting a go at his own competition.

Georgie made another contribution, "What

about the Spring Flights" he said, "There were three of them!!"

"They were four Blue Arrows!" the gruff old voice of St.Sampsons Bill had finally joined the game.

"Crumbs! you're going back a bit there Bill," said Artie, "That was before the war."

"Nobody said we couldn't go back before the war," argued Bill.

"Ah well!! in that case," said Charlie, his lap full of suspicious black crumbs, "In that case, what about the Lady Kathleen."

"And the Celia," said Artie.

"I remember before the war," a quiet dreamy voice floated across the room, as Ernies mind had decided to rejoin the human race after its celestial visit to far away galaxies, "I remember before the war, there were two Herm boats, one was called MISS - I - CAN - GO, and the other was MISS - I - CAN - GO - FASTER."

That was a conversation stopper if ever I heard one. Georgie and I wouldn't be old enough to know one way or the other if this statement was right, and the ones who were old enough to know, were all looking from one to the other with puzzled expressions.

"I don't remember those," said Artie, "What about you Charlie."

Charlie was shaking his head.

"Well! I know one thing," said gruff Bill, "It's no good asking me, - - - you'll all know more about these things than me - - - being townies."

"You've all forgotten Newtons Ferries," said Georgie suddenly, Ben Gunn, Martha Gunn, Newton Gazelle, Clacton Gazelle, and the Henry Rose 11."

"By heck!" said Stan, "You've really picked a character there, 'ol Bonnie Newton, he were priceless, 'ol Bonnie. The Blue Arrows you were on about Bill, they were his, mind you it wasn't before the war, he didn't start them 'till 1947. Before that he was too busy being a war hero!"

"What really?" I asked intrigued.

"Oh yes!" said Stan, "He was in the Royal Naval reserve and got himself attached to the S.O.E. for the commando raid on the Casquets lighthouse, he piloted the landing craft. They captured the seven man garrison, there wasn't many who knew the rocks around there better than Bonnie. He was awarded the D.S.C. the Croix de Guerre and palm and Silver Star!"

"What a Guernseyman awarded the Croix de Guerre?" I asked surprised.

"An Alderneyman, an Alderneyman," said Stan with mock indignation.

"Well you know what I mean!" I said laughing.

"Anyway," said Charlie suddenly, "Why wouldn't a Guernseyman receive the Croix de Guerre?"

"We've had men from this Island receive every conceivable medal, infact Wallace Le Patourel was awarded the V.C. for bravery in North Africa." Everyone was looking at him by now so he continued. "In a place called Tabourba it was, all his mates had been killed and he stormed a gun emplacement single handed. Oh yes," he said finally, "You don't have to worry about Guernseymen, we're not behind the wall when it comes to medals."

"I know one who should have had the Nazi iron cross," mumbled grumpy Bill.

I thought oh no! not again!! this was yet

another reference to the bloke who shopped him to the Germans for stealing chickens during the Occupation. I looked across at Georgie, he had turned his eyes up towards the ceiling, in a 'not the bloney chicken story again' expression.

Before it could go any further Stan leaned forward, and moved to the edge of the seat.

"I can tell you a story about Bonnie," he smiled, and he had everyones attention. "You remember when the Briseis went down.

"Art does," said Georgie with a grin. Everyone laughed, everybody except Artie, he was warm, so he was aleep.

Stan pressed on, "Well the day she went down, Bonnie and Hubert Petit found four of the barrels floating off the coast. Being public spirited, they handed one of them in to the authorities," everyone laughed again, - - - - one. "Then after that they proceeded to spend the rest of the day drinking the contents of another. Finally after it was dark they went ashore in Herm and buried the other two. The trouble was they drank so much of the remaining barrel, that from that day to this neither of them have ever --- remembered where they buried the barrels."

Well! as you can imagine everyone laughed heartily at that, so heartily that Artie woke up.

"What's up?" he asked, "Whats up?"

Before I could tell him, 'ol Ernie started in the corner.

"Well Bless us and save us, who'd have thought we'd live to see the day, it's young Barry." Barry was one of the plumbers, and was as Bill would say, 'Stans nipper.'

"Where on earth have you been in this lot? said Ernie, "You're covered in snow. Get here by the stove," everyone made way for him to get warm.

"I've been out to the Catioroc," said Barry rubbing his hands in front of the stove.

"What? to see our famous actor," said Charlie chuckling.

"Yes, seriously," said Barry, "He had a dripping tap!"

Charlie looked surprised. "Did you see Barry Jones himself then?" he asked.

"I did better than that, who do you think answered the door."

"Somebody famous ?" queried Charlie.

"Yep, well known in Hollywood!"

"Give us a clue," said Ernie. So Barry began.

"When I got there I rang the bell, the door opened. I said I was the plumber, and this man beckoned me inside, and in a creepy voice he said; 'Come this way I'll show you the demon that kept me awake all night.' Drip . . . Drip . . . Drip . . . he was really spooky.

"Go on then," said Charlie, "Who was it?"

"ALFRED HITCHCOCK!"

"Get away with you," said Ernie, "It would be all over the press if he was here."

"Not necessarily," said Georgie, "I've heard he's had loads of Hollywood friends to stay with him at the Catioroc. They just fly in under an assumed name and stay on holiday with him."

"He's made some good horror films that Alfred Hitchcock," said Charlie.

"I like Boris Karlof best," said Ernie.

"Do you know his brother lives at the old mill, St.Martins," said Stan.

"Get away with you," said Ernie, "There's no Karlofs living in Guernsey."

"Ah!" said Stan, "But their family name isn't Karlof, it's Pratt and his brother does live at the old mill."

I have to say here, that it was awfully hard with these lunchtime stories to tell what was real and what wasn't. But fact being stranger than fiction, I believe that what Stan said on this occasion was true.

"Listen!" said Barry, finally starting to thaw out from his ride in the snow, "Have you heard about El, at the tax office last week?"

Ernie was laughing already, he loved stories about our Elvis.

"No! seriously," said Barry, "This is absolutely true. El had to go to the tax office last week, and the woman behind the counter realizing that El wasn't too hot on the reading and writing led him through into a little cubicle so she could help him fill in his form. The first line said full name, so she filled in that line. The next was address, so he told her his address, she did that, then she said to him occupation: -- He pulled himself up to his full height and said:-- I stayed here, all the way through - - - I didn't go running off to England like all those others."

Well everyone roared with laughter, but Ernie got into such a state he rolled right off the bench, it seemed ages before he could get his breath back enough to say, with a bright red face and wet eyes;

"Eeee -- that Elvis, he's as daft as a brush!!"

CHAPTER ELEVEN

THE OTHER SQUARE THAT ISN'T

In thinking about how Trinity Square is really a triangle, I couldn't help thinking that Town church square doesn't really exist at all. Having said that, the area around the town church was awash with great characters, especially in the days of Dodd's Popular Cafe. I can still remember on the outside wall near the door a marvellous picture painted of a tea-pot on legs, with a cheeky face, raising his lid to passers by and the quote underneath, 'Mr. T.Pott recommends the Popular.

I suppose the first face that springs to mind, pacing up and down in front of the church is Happy Snaps Sue, the girl who must have taken thousands of photos over the years, come on now!! Be honest most of you have got at least one in the family album that was taken by Sue. In my minds eye I can go back to those far-off sunny summer days, when the three little De Bourgonniere brothers would lean on the Balastrade at the bottom of Cornet

Street facing the church, each one identically dressed in grey flannel trousers, navy blue guernseys, and blue 'bounnet' (or pom pom hat without the pom pom). They were Alphonse, Francios, and Mocot, and as my old Dad used to say, it is a little known historical fact of the Channel Islands that Guernsey was discovered by 'phonse De Bourgonniere whilst digging for bait on Castle Cornet. Complete with his two sticks, I remember Henry Poullain. On another occasion I was passing the old green bench seat that used to be in front of the church railings facing the Herm ferry slipway, when I had the opportunity to photograph not one, but two of our well known town characters together. One was Len Brache and the second was that other well known newspaper seller and rival to Billy Roswell, Harold Guillou. How many times as boys did we call out to Harold, 'Paper Boy - Paper Boy,' and wait for his indignant reply: -

"Paper Man!!"

Speaking of the Herm ferry slipway, who can remember the lady who everyday went down to feed the first little white duck with the orange beak that suddenly arrived one day in the harbour? She became so famous for feeding the new arrival she even appeared on Channel Television!! It was a great slipway for ferries. I used to like it when they were moored three or four abreast, and you sometimes had to climb from one to the other across the seats until you were in your right one. Great characters of that slipway of course would have to include Herbie Renouf, along with Bonnie, another old hand at the game.

John tells a great little story from these days. He said he was helping out on one of the ferries doing the odd evening trips. This particular evening they had taken a boat load of visitors to Herm for the evening, and whilst the passengers had a wander around the Island, they went into the Mermaid for a couple of pints. After about an hour two grey haired old ladies appeared at the door of the pub, John recognised them as two of his passengers and asked if there was anything wrong.

"Well," said one old dear, "We've been right to the top of the hill and we can't find the bus stop anywhere!"

By this time the general babble of conversation had died right down, as John asked;

"What bus stop?"

"Well," she said, "Our friends told us, when you get off the boat, take a steady walk to the top of the hill and you'll see the bus stop. If you wait there the bus will bring you back down into St.Peter Port."

Nobody in the bar laughed, but John says there were some pretty big grins, and some must have been biting their lip, as it began to dawn on everyone that the two old dears had come all the way to Herm thinking they were on the Fermain boat.

Another great town character I remember was 'Bow leg Jock' as his name suggests he wasn't a donkey, but a great little Scot usually wearing a Tam-o-shanter. His legs were so bowed that he used to walk with his hands on his thighs.

Another lady from the seats in front of the town church was 'Pheobie' Stonebridge whose husband was that 'happy clown' George, who could be seen dressed in his costume at Cavalcades, and the North Show and anywhere he could entertain the crowd.

Talking of the North Show, there was a lady who often entered the fancy dress section as an old Guernsey woman in costume, complete with old Guernsey Bonnet, and whilst so dressed she also played the accordian. She was Mary Le Sauvage.

Going back to Pheobie she loved to chat with anyone and everyone, and I had a bit of bad luck one afternoon. I went to a matinee performance at the Odeon. I past Pheobie sitting near the back, I said hello as always, and went and sat half way down. Not more than a minute into the film a beautiful girl came onto the screen, and Pheobie called to me from the back;

"Look at her, look how pretty she is, and to think that wicked swine kills her."

Pheobie had seen the film before, and within a minute of the start she'd wrecked the plot, and I had just thrown a couple of quid down the drain. You have to laugh!!

I wonder if I could stretch my town church

square area to include the market, because there were good friends in there. One was called 'Coll' Richards where I used to get the family meat every Saturday. Another was that very strong meat porter Fred Ruff. He could carry the meat, a half a cow at a time, 'till the whole shipment was cleared. In the fish market was a lady I liked very much, and that was Mrs.Mauger. I can still see her in my minds eye filleting fish so fast, she made others look like non-starters. I remember speaking about her one night when someone said to me; - - - -

"She was a big lady."

I naturally agreed, I said, "She was a big lady."

Then this person said, "Do you know what she weighed?"

I said, "No - I have no idea."

They said - - - "Fish!!"

Well I suppose I walked into that one!

When we first moved into our new home, which was a very old cottage with marvellous outhouses and sheds. There was all sorts of stuff left in them, and amongst it all was an old wind-up gramophone Because the age of the old 78s was almost gone, there was only two record shops left selling them, and also the little tins of gramophone needles. One was just below the Normandie Beer Gardens in Le Febvre Street and the other was Basil Mecklereid in Mansell Street, a couple of doors up from Bisson's Army and Navy stores. It was a great old record shop full of character, sheet music all around cheap records Box, and Basil himself was very knowledgeable having been in the trade for so many years. Speaking of which I heard a radio interview one day with a man who was retiring after a lifetime in a record shop, and he was speaking of the changes he'd seen, and so on. The interviewer asked;

"Do you remember any funny incidents that have stuck in your mind over the years?"

The old chap said, "Well we've had some unusual requests from time to time, but the least information I've ever had to go on was an elderly lady who came in here one afternoon, and asked for a record."

"Its not for me you understand," she said, "Its for my young neice, I'm not sure what its called, but its by somebody or others 'Carbuncle,' and its about some trouble over in Bridgewater."

What I thought was marvellous, is that from this the old boy ascertained which one she wanted !!

To return to Town church square, another local character who must be mentioned was the 'Town Crier,' Roy Finch. After a lifetime of helping young lads away from a wasted life of crime, in his position as local probation officer, he then sportingly had a go as the town crier, bringing not only a powerful clear voice, but I felt, a touch of dignity to the role. What about 'Curly Martin' another great townie. Up at the crack of dawn, cleaning the huge shop windows, in all weathers, summer and winter. Never giving a thought to the luxury of retirement, 'till 1988 when he finally thought maybe I should now in this my eightieth year.

Another of the more recent characters was Percy Le Poidevin, the lottery ticket man in the electric wheelchair, usually parked by the post office at the bottom of market steps. John 'The Canary' Sarre, was a Torteval man who used to become a temporary townie each year in the days leading up to Christmas when he would play the Christmas carols on his accordian, in the doorway of the former Fletchers sports shop, opposite the House of Bellingham travel agents in the arcade.

And last but not least I must include the much loved Peter Legg, the transistor radio man. Peter a roadsweeper of many years can often be seen, when off duty in the summer, around the local beauty spots and beaches with as many as four or five radios, very often all tuned to different stations.

When the Gaumont closed down Radio Guernsey interviewed a lady usherette of 30 years service, asking her if she had any funny things happen over the years. She recalled the evening she and the manager thought the front row was on fire, smoke could be seen rising in front of the screen lights. They rushed down there only to find a young man slouched well down in the seat with a big brown bean jar on his lap, and eating the steaming contents with a tablespoon. That was Peter!! Its like he says;

"Who needs ice-cream and nuts, when you

can have bean jar?"

With one last look at the ferry slip in front of the town church, and one last recalling of the ferry skippers such as Percy Ferguson on the Fermain boats, and going back to ol' Freddie Zabelia who had the 'Celia', I must close with two little pearls of Freds. One was when some people were winding him up saying;

"We don't know if it's safe to go with you, if you don't know where all the rocks are."

And Fred said," I know something even better than that, I know where they're not."

The other was when he got a whole boat load trying to guess what is the most dangerous sea creature of them all, and after many varied guesses, he said;

"Its the limpet," whilst all the amazed faces stared at him, he said, "Because if you hit one of those, you know your in serious - serious trouble."

CHAPTER TWELVE

BOBBYS AND HUMOUR

In my early days at the 'Stalag' whilst I was still a cyclist, I had occasion to ride my bicycle down Les Val de Terres, about halfway down I heard a motor bike behind me and made up my mind to beat it to the bottom. Coming down the Terres it's surprising the advantage a push bike has over a motor bike, having very little weight, thin frame etc. One can throw it around all the curves quicker, and as I was approaching the Guernsey Brewery at the bottom, I was giving myself a mental pat on the back for having stayed ahead. As I was passing the gardens on the left the motor cycle pulled level, as I was staring into the grinning face of Noel Trotter. Because the speed limit down the Terres at the time was about 15 M.P.H. my heart sank.

He said, "Pull over."

I said, "Yes it is nice my Mum knitted it," - - - - but he wasn't having any of it !! I think he'd heard them all before, so I had to stop.

"My My," he said, "What have we here? did it fall out of a Christmas cracker ?"

I said, "It's a good bike !"

Only those of you who can remember how close his dry wit came to sarcasm can imagine his voice when he said;

"Oh yes ! and so fast as well."

Well by this time I figured I was in trouble anyway, so made the serious mistake of getting cheeky.

I said, "Well it was fast enough to beat you down the hill !"

"Yes," he said, " It certainly was ! The only thing I found with that model is, there not so fast going back up !!"

As the full implication began to dawn, I said, " AGHH you wouldn't ?"

" Oh wouldn't I ?" he said, " and when you get half way up and you think, silly Mr. Trotter's gone, I'll be riding around - - - watching - - and - - - waiting."

I had to push the blinking bike all the way to the top, he never did come back, but with Noel, you could never be sure.

Dave Le Page got stopped by Noel when he

was a teenage motor cyclist, Noel left him in no doubt about his speed in regard to the law of the land, and finished up by saying - - - -

"This is your very very last warning."

Dave realising that Noel had mistaken him for someone else said, " But this is my first warning."

"That's what I mean," said Noel, - - - "You only get one !!"

In the days when you could ride down Victoria Road, my mate Garry and I were going down on our way to town just around dusk, a car coming up forced me into the granite cobbled gutter, all the bouncing caused the top of the cycle lamp to fly off and the battery bounced out and smashed to pieces on the pavement. The lamp had stayed where it was, so I retrieved the top and placed it on the lamp, off we went again when we got down into Fountain Street, out stepped uncle Noel.

"Well then," he said, "Where's your lights ?"

I started to explain, " I was coming down Victoria Road," - - - that was as far as I got, he put up his hand to silence me, he said;

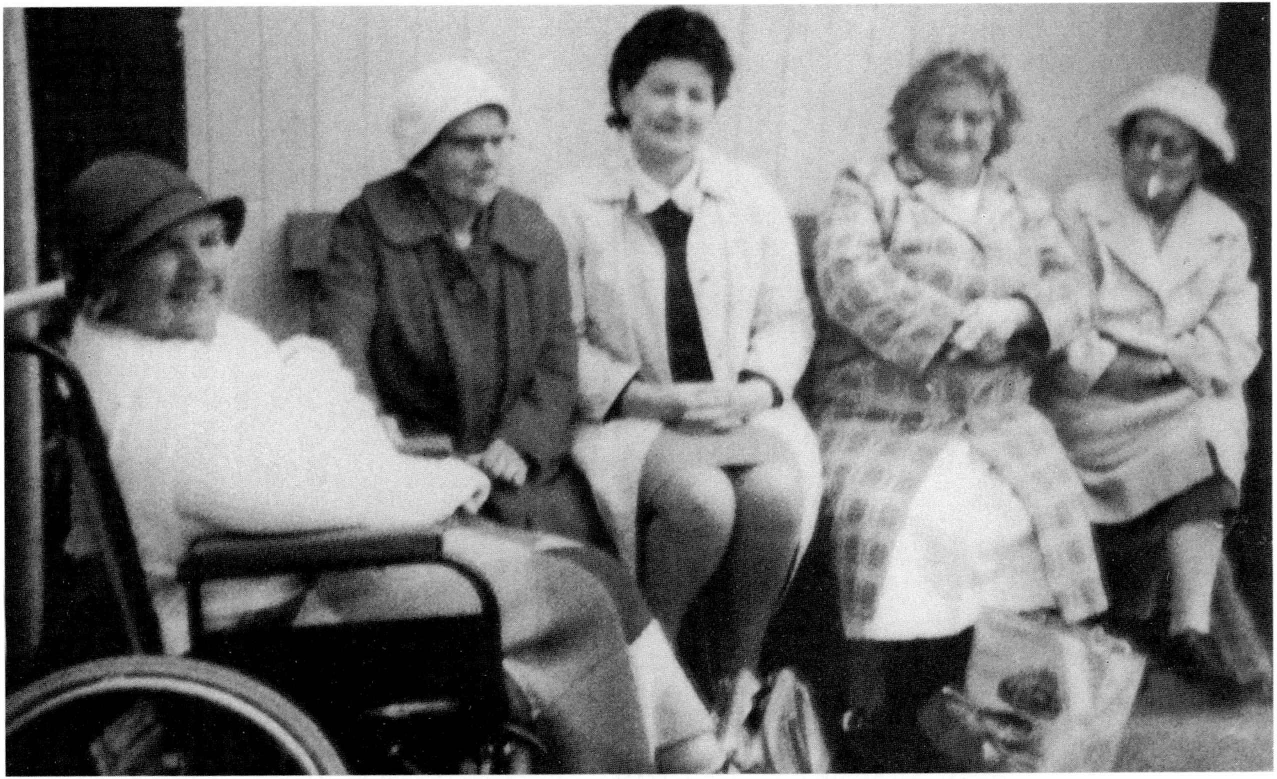

HILDA, EVA, RUTH, MAY & GRAN FISHER

SAM DRUEE

CHARLIE & MAUDIE PENGELLEY

ETHEL

GRANDES ROCQUES WILF

STAN OGIER

COLLI RICHARDS

MRS MAUGER

"Don't tell me, don't tell me, let me guess, - - it all, - - - jumped ! - out."

Garry went into hysterics, I was left speechless, I was standing looking at him with my mouth open, because in one outburst of sarcasm he had actually said, what had really happened. The fact that Garry was crying with laughter convinced Noel, that whatever I was going to say, would have been a pack of lies anyway. A few days later I was able to laugh about it along with Garry, but not that night. That night I was back to pushing the blinkin' bike again.

Noel's three contemporary motorcycle patrol officers were all called Peter. There was Peter Rabey, Peter Castle and Peter Falla. When some years ago I had a job that sent me daily to fetch the post in Forest Lane, I would often meet up with Peter Castle, by then retired from the force and like me with a job that included fetching the post. If, as sometimes happened the post was late, (Due, as Graham would say, to not being able to get the pigeon down off the roof), we would exchange stories about old Guernsey characters. One day he was trying to illustrate how difficult it can be getting the balance just right between being a good policeman and a good husband and father. He told the following story; "One night I was on duty on the 10pm 'till 6am shift. At 9 o'clock the following morning we, as a family, were flying out on the start of our fortnight annual holiday. At around midnight I found myself following an old car along Cobo Coast Road, and it was drifting from side to side across the road. Now I was faced with a dilemma, if I ignored him and he went on to have an accident and possibly even killed someone, I couldn't really call myself a copper at all. If on the other hand I booked him he would have to appear before the Magistrate at 10am in the morning, and me with him, thereby wrecking the families holiday."

I interrupted him at this point, and asked, "How on earth did you get around a problem like that ?"

"Well," he said, "I pulled him over by Maryland Garage and said you've had a few tonight Pop!"

He slurred back, "Your bloomin right there

shir, I've shcertainly 'ad a few tonight."

I explained to him how serious it was to drive in that condition. Then I asked where he lived.

He said, "Fort Richmond."

I said, "Now I'm going to tell you what we're going to do, get in the passengers seat," and I hid my patrol bike down Cobo slip, behind the wall. Then I got in and drove him all the way to Richmond, then of course I had to drive up the bumpy cart track to the Fort itself. When I'd parked up he got out and I made sure the car was securely locked, and then I went over to him in the pitch dark and I said, "I want you to give me your word that you will never ever drive in that condition ever again."

He said, "Yesh shir I promise, and I am shorry, and it won't happen again."

With that I placed his ignition keys in his hand, and as I was walking away in the dark, I turned back and said, "By the way, you do know who I am?"

He said, "No shir."

I said - "And don't you ever try to find out!"

Then came the long walk back to Cobo.

This of course would not be possible in this day and age with constant radio contact, although the modern force is not without amusing incidents. There's a lovely story about a freezing cold night when the two foot patrol policemen came upon the patrol car with two other policemen inside, hiding out of the way in Park Street. Being such a cold night they climbed in the back for a bit of a chat and a warm up. Human nature being what it is, as they warmed up, all four of them became drowsy and eventually fell asleep, they might have been found like that in the morning except that at 3am the constable in the front passenger seat, thinking he was home in bed, turned over! driving his knee into the siren switch. What followed must have been wonderful to see. With the blue lights flashing and the sirens screaming, the two in the back who had no business anywhere near the car were fighting each other to get out of the back door. In this sudden pandemonium, lights in Park Street, Rue du Pre and even Cour du Parc flats were being flicked on all over the show.

The driver was desperately trying to locate the ignition keys, whilst his trouble causing passenger struggled in the dark to find the offending switch.

The next fifteen minutes were spent driving around expecting a radio report of a flood of phone calls, but the rest of the shift passed off quietly, much to everyone's relief.

I suppose over all, we have been quite fortunate with our local force, there usually being just about enough fair ones to make up, for the dictatorial ones. Even so I still had to smile when I read recently on a St. Peter Port wall, 'Support your local police, beat yourself up!'

It seems to me that there is humour with a local twist in almost all aspects of life, like the famous old proverb: 'Red sky at night, donkey's delight.' (It means Jersey's on fire).

It goes back to our childhood, when we were told marvellous fairy stories, like Snow White cleaning her neat little house, when all the villagers came rushing up on their way to the diamond mines, there had been a rock fall and the seven dwarfs were trapped. Snow

White went with them, people were scrambling amongst the rocks and debris in the dust filled mine. Suddenly a man at the back, listening carefully heard a voice very faintly singing Jerseys going to win the Muratti, Jerseys going to win the Muratti.

"Quick over here, everyone lend a hand, dopey's still alive!"

Some people have said that we donkeys are tight fisted, or even mean with our money, but that is grossly unfair. We are careful, very, very, very careful. When Bert Tosteven died, his wife went down to the Guernsey Evening Press office to enter the sad fact in the Hatches - Matches - and Dispatches. When she inquired how much, the lady at the desk explained, it was X amount for the initial insert and so much a word after that.

"Oh!" said Mrs.Bert, "So much a word. - - - Well look! put 'Tosty Dead!"

The woman looked at her in amazement, she said, "That's a bit brief, isn't it?"

"Well," she said, "That's what his mates call him, and that's what happened."

So the lady tried again, she said, "Look! you

get five words for the initial insert alone."

"Ahh," said Mrs.Bert, "Five words, ah well, that's different, in that case put Tosty dead Volvo for sale!"

This carefulness, was even considered proof enough in a court case one time. Two men from St.Peters were in court charged with drunk and disorderly. The Magistrate asked, "How do you know they were drunk?"

The prosecuting officer said, "Well sir, one of them was dropping his money on the ground and the other one was picking it up and giving it back to him."

"Ah yes," said the Magistrate, "Yes Guilty!"

Incidently, of all the versions I've heard of how Tosty came to meet his untimely demise, I think the least likely to be the one that said, he went to the local pet shop and bought the two biggest budgerigars in the place, paid for them cash, then drove to the fire station at the town Arsenal, got the key to the Victoria Tower from the duty sergeant, climbed the spiral staircase right to the top, stepped out onto the battlement, tucked a bird under each arm and leapt off. Taking a downward flight with all the areodynamic gracefulness of a house-brick. He plunged into the ground at a rapid rate of knots. A person nearby, who had seen everything, raced over to him in time to hear him with his last breath utter those immortal lines:- "Demmie, this budgie jumping aint all it's cracked up to be, eh?"

Those who enjoyed the stories of Reggie Lamb in my first book, 'Donkey's ears Ago' will be sorry to learn that since I originally started that book, Reg suffered a serious stroke. However you will no doubt be very glad to hear he is making a good steady recovery. He gets around, taking drives out around the Island with his dear wife Pat. I saw her recently at Pembroke and of course immediately inquired after Reg.

"Oh," she said, "He's down at the end, sitting on the bonnet of the car, go and have a chat with him, I'm just going to walk the dog." Sure enough I found Reg sitting enjoying the day.

"Waddo Reg."

"Waddo mate, how you doing?"

"I'm doing alright, but I heard you had a

stroke."

"Yeah, this time last year they thought they were going to have to cremate me." Then he winked, and nudged me with his elbow and said, "But no roast lamb yet."

Didn't I laugh, he seems to be happy and mucking about all the time. I said, "I Just saw Pat, she told me you were here."

"Ah," he said, "ol' Pat Bless her, I lost her y'know."

I immediately suspected another Reggie special was coming. I said, "How do you mean lost her?"

He said, "She ran off with some bloke!"

"What! - Pat?" I said in fake astonishment.

"Yeah, she ran off with some bloke one night, and I had to report it to the police station. I said to the desk sergeant, Pat's run off with someone."

He said to me, "Come on Reg, wipe that smile off your face."

I said, "Well I had to come and report it."

The sergeant said, "You don't look too upset about it all."

I said, "No -- there's no need for me to get

upset, when he sees her in the daylight, -- he'll bring her back!!"

I was laughing again, it was just good to be back in his company. Reg has a knack of very quickly seeing the potential for fun in any given situation. I mean one thing I've seen him do many times yet the element of surprise still makes me laugh. He will walk away from a group of people very quickly, with a - 'I've got work to do, I can't hang about here all day.' Followed immediately by a trip then a stumble then he regains his balance goes straight back to the offending item, picks it up, and waving it in front of all and sundry rants on and on about the selfish inconsiderations of wicked people who throw these things down willy nilly, without any thought for anyone else. And everyone ends up laughing because in your heart of hearts you know it's an awful lot of fuss to make over a spent matchstick.

It's a knack, I must confess I've only seen equalled by one other local character, and that was Fred 'The Gas' Page. If I could give an example of this. I was giving a talk on local characters one evening, when a lady in the group recalled, that when she first came to the Island from Wales thirty years before, her first job was at the gas company. She spoke of the suspense and fun, wondering what Fred would do when he entered the building each time. She said one of the first things she ever saw him do was walk straight over to a pile of newspapers that he had just spotted in the corner, took one of them and crumpled it up into a wad, made a hole in the middle and immediately began eating chips out of it. Not only that, but he began to offer them to everyone around him. She said, what was amazing was the speed with which everybody joined in the fun. -- Have a chip, -- Have a chip, then one man who dug his hand in with a -- thanks very much Fred, got his hand slapped. I said have a chip, not the fish, the fish is mine. Wonderful fun. Some say he went too far, but I only ever heard of one lady complaining to the company, apparently just before lunch one day. The lady of the house asked Fred, how much pipe do you think you'll need for this job.

"Oh, I don't know really," said Fred, "Hang

on I'll measure." So he went out to his van parked in the the road and came back with a piece of string. "There you are," he said, "Just keep your finger on one end." He took it halfway along the wall and said, "No, that's no good, just hang on a bit," and went out again to his van. After twenty minutes she finally let go of her end, went and looked out of the window, and of course both Fred and the van had gone to lunch! I must admit to biting my lip, even at this one.

To return to Reggie, I wouldn't want anyone to think that Pat is always on the receiving end of the jokes and stories. She can more than hold her own in this department, and so to date still holds, in my opinion, the best of all time award for the one I heard from the nursing staff at the King Edward. Some months after Reggie's stroke when he was gradually getting better and stronger, and was attending physiotherapy sessions to get the strength back in the affected limbs. One of the sessions coincided with Pat's birthday.

Naturally all the staff wished her happy birthday, and one of them asked her what she would like. Pat shrugged and laughed she said, "Aw, I'm not bothered over much about presents and all that."

But the nurse persisted, "Go on Pat -- if you could have anything in the world, what would you like?"

She cocked her head on one side, thought about it seriously for a moment, then with a wicked grin, said, "A widows pension!!"

She brought the place down, even Reggie ended up with a stitch laughing at that one.

In Donkey's Ears Ago, I tried to recapture some of the nostalgia of the old greenhouse steaming, and my final story about Reg happened when he and a mate were steaming nights. Steaming with grids as opposed to pans, often led the vinery owner to worry whether the men had dug down deep enough for the most effective use of the steam. However the grower Reg was working for was so tight that he was practically spying on their every move. His trips down the greenhouse to make sure everything was alright, coincided with the end of almost every cook. So, as the next trench was being prepared, he would suddenly appear in the mist & steam and say, 'Make sure she's deep enough boys, make sure she's deep enough.' (This would give you a depth of approx 2½ feet).

Reg was in the trench one night digging when he caught sight of him making his way, yet again, from the top of the greenhouse. With a wink, Reg said to his mate watch this and dropped to his knees in the trench. As the owner came through the billowing steam, all he could see was the tip of Reggie's shovel throwing ground up onto the top of the heep. He was practically screaming when he raced forward, waving his hands in the air.

"Oh no boys - No boys - No, Not that deep!!"

It was then that Reggie stood up again grinning.

The owner said, "You Rascal," he must have been a methodist), "You really scared me that time," and after that he only came around once a night until the job was done!

CHAPTER THIRTEEN

VRAIC -- SEAWEED TO YOU

P.P. one, two, two, said Ernie. We were all in our cosy positions around the stove again, Charlies sandwich was already in place, smouldering nicely. Artie had asked the question, what was the name of the sea-plane that crashed outside the town harbour. I'd said it was an R.A.F. Sunderland flying boat, and right out of the blue Ernie announced the registration number. These little flashes of brilliance used to amaze me because half the time, one suspected that he couldn't remember his own name, then suddenly 'P.P.122.'

"Do you remember it," asked Art.

I nodded, "Yeah, my Dad took me and my sister to see it in the careening hard. They even let us go on board. I had a turn in the pilots seat playing with the joy stick."

"Is that the earliest thing you remember?"

"No, I remember when all the mackerel came in, the year before, and the Queens Coronation. We all had a mug and a navy blue tin with the Queens head on, and a bar of chocolate inside. I can remember when we still had a ration book for sweets, and my Dad took us down to see Dorey's boat The Fermain on the rocks opposite the Vale Castle."

"He remembers the Fermain," said old Albie with a sneer. Albie was nearing retirement age and was more often out on boiler maintenance. "He remembers the Fermain," he tutted a few times. "I remember the Swansea!"

"Get away with you," said Ernie, "That was the turn of the century."

"July 1906, she hit Les Grune Rocks, they towed her into Vazon Bay. I was six years old and my father took me down to see her. They were unloading the coal to make her lighter and repairing the hole, eventually they re-floated her. I remember it as though it were yesterday."

"Dearie me, today next week, who'd 'ave thought we'd live to see the day -- the old Swansea. Well bless us and save us you've shook me there Albie."

He'd shook me an' all. I imagined that anyone who could go back to 1906 should be able to remember the ark as well.

"I think your lunch might be ready Charlie," Albie mumbled, nodding towards the stove. The sandwich had not only turned, as it frequently did, the colour of jet, but instead of catching fire, this time it had solidified and shrunk to take on the size and appearance of a congealed, black toasted matchbox.

"Ah! thanks," said Charlie, and ate it.

"Talking about Vazon," said Stan, "Guess who I saw out there yesterday?"

All eyes looked across at him, some with eyebrows raised expectantly.

"Seaweed Joe!"

"Well," said Ernie, "If you saw him at Vazon, he was off his usual patch, he's a Perelle man is Seaweed Joe."

"What's his real name?" I asked, "Joe what?"

"It's not Joe at all," said Ernie, " It's Fred! Frederick Brehaut, he collects vriac, loads it on his handcart and takes it home."

I was curious by now, "What's he do with it there?" I asked.

"Burns it in the fireplace, good cheap fuel! and that's not all, when he cleans out the ash in the morning, he puts it in sacks and sells it to the growers as potash, makes good fertilizer."

"Potash?" Charlie queried, "Potash? I thought they made Iodine from burnt seaweed."

"They do," said Stan, "As potash it makes a good fertilizer, and as Iodine it makes a good Anti-septic. Up until the war there was an Iodine factory on Lihou Island."

"I remember it," said Albie.

Well to be quite honest, I wasn't surprised, anyone who could remember the Swansea, was likely to remember anything.

"There was one in the Steam Mill lanes as well," said Stan.

"One what?" asked Charlie.

"Another Iodine factory," said Stan.

"I don't think so," answered Charlie, in an argumentative voice, "I don't remember that."

"Well there was," Stan insisted, "If you came into the Steam Mill lanes from the Rue Poudreuse end, it was halfway down the lane on the right hand side."

"There's no point in asking me," said happy

Bill, "I wouldn't know, I'm a St.Sampsons man, me, Born and Bred!"

"I can remember at school," Charlie started again, "When the kids would all be walking about with purple patches on their heads from that stuff."

"No - No," said Ernie, "That wouldn't be Iodine, would it Stan?"

"No," answered Stan, "The purple stuff is called Genetian Violet, it does a similar job, but Iodine is more browny orangie colour."

"Ochre," said Ernie.

"Alright," laughed Stan, "If you're going to be posh, 'Ochre'!"

Georgie, who had been remarkably quiet during this particular discussion looked across at Ernie and said, "Wasn't it Iodine that you once said was stored in a massive tank on the Crown Pier."

Ernie looked at him completely bewildered.

"You said it was some sort of liquid Anti septic," Georgie continued, "You know people took their containers down to be filled."

"Ah, - No -No, now I know what you're on about, that was thallasol, that was more a disinfectant come bleach, the women used to scrub the house down with thallasol, especially the ol' front doorstep."

"Only I thought you said," continued George, "That it was made from seaweed as well."

"No - No," said Ernie, "Sea water not seaweed, it was made from sea water."

"How?" asked George.

"Ah - you got me there," Ernie replied, "All I remember was old Pop Le Goupillot was in charge, and inside the store that the tank sat on. Sea water used to pass over some metal plates, in some sort of electrolysis system."

"Is that the building," asked George, "That stands on the top of the careening hard where the beach reaches the road?" (Now replaced by toilets).

"Yes that's the one," Ernie nodded.

"I remember before the war," commenced Albie, "It was the common practice for the states treasurer and one assistant, from time to time, to take all the local currency notes which had been withdrawn from circulation across the road from the states office, into the careening hard, and tip them out in a heap in the corner by the thallasol store and make themselves a very expensive bonfire." You can be sure that Albie had everyones attention with this story.

They discontinued this practice after a mishap, to wit, before the flames could get a good start one morning, a gust of wind took the heap for a sight seeing tour of St.Peter Port. Ten bobs, pounds and fivers all over the town, - - - - By heck, there was some poor people eating well that week.

"It seems to me," said a sleepy voice from under a large cap, "It seems to me, that if the medical fraternity still uses loads of Iodine in many different forms, and the growing fraternity still uses loads of potash fertilizers, and we've got tons and tons of vraic on the west coast, and people unemployed, it wouldn't be out of the way for someone to put up a factory with a furnace. --- You'd probably need a covered drying area with racks or something, like an elongated dutch barn, once it was dry bung it in the furnace."

Everyone was sitting there nodding, it was

amazing what Artie could come out with sometimes.

"The trouble is," said Stan, "If it was being done on a large scale, you might have to use thousands of gallons of fresh water constantly to be clearing the salt content."

"Well," said Artie again, "If - - -

"Skylark," said Ernie.

Everyone looked at him mystified.

"Skylark," he said again, "You remember last week all the Herm ferries, no one thought of the Skylark."

"What is he on about?" asked Albie, looking around.

"Last week," said Artie, not in the least upset that Ernie had cut him off mid sentence, "Last week, I asked how many Herm ferry names we could remember."

Albie who hadn't been there on the day in question, replied with, -- "Oh yes, and did anyone remember the Merry Widow."

People were shaking their heads, confirming what he'd suspected.

"Fancy forgetting her," he said, "Don't you know what the big book says, not to forget about the widows or the fatherless!"

"The fatherless?" said dry Ernie, "Are you sure Albie, I don't remember one called the fatherless."

"Perhaps," said the dormouse, "She was a Sark boat."

Everyone laughed. I looked across at happy Bill, he had a face like a Bulldog chewing a wasp. I could see that because he wasn't the centre of attention, he was itching to break up the party.

"Been to Otto?" This question was directed at George, who had all the hall marks of a recent haircut.

"No," he said, "I went to Minier, you know opposite Le Rays chip shop at the top of Contree Mansell."

"What were you doing in that neck of the woods?" asked Stan.

"I had to go to Adams, the little electrical shop next door, to fetch an accumalator for my grans wireless, so I nipped in and had a haircut while I was there."

"Contree Mansell eh?" said Ernie, "I bet you could smell the chemmies crisps frying there."

"Ah well," came a grumpy voice from the other side of the stove, "I suppose we'll have to."

CHAPTER FOURTEEN

WHEN HARRY STOLE THE BUS

You may have read in the press about Harry stealing the bus, and I know what you're thinking, why would anyone who can't even drive a car steal a bus? The trouble is, you're using standard logic, and Harry logic works completely different. Harry logic says here we are, me and my mate, in the Red Lion. We're half cut, we're living right up by the Castel church, we've got no transport, and the bus garage is only fifty yards down the road. Down they went, Harry went in, his mate stayed as lookout.

His mate takes up the story. "I'm outside keeping an eye an' I can hear Harry inside banging about. A bus door opened, an engine started up, moved a couple of feet, engine off, door slammed shut, another opened, engine started up, back a bit, switched off. It was bedlam in there, engines being started, stopped, doors banging, at one point I was peering in through the gloom and I saw Harry passing. I said, "Hey Harry what's going on?"

He said, "ain't it just our luck, we live right up by the Castel church an' the number sixteen is right at the back!"

* * * * * * * * * * *

THE LEGENDRY DOG FIGHT

In a well known local pub, famous for its large rear car park, nudge - nudge, you know which one, wink - wink, -- say no more.

There was for many years, a very aggravating local, with a very vicious pit bull terrier. At some time or other, all the other locals had either had their dogs savaged or lost money on someone else's dogs attempt to beat this beast. Needless to say he was not a popular man, and it was with some joy that the locals heard a very encouraging statement from a quiet stranger in the bar. Having listened for some time to this man boasting and bragging about his dogs prowess, the quiet stranger said;

"I think mine could beat it."

"What raged the man, going purple in the face, how dare you, my pit bull terrier can - - - - - - What kind have you got anyway?"

"It's called," said the stranger quietly, "A long nose, long tailed, short legged terrier."

"What!" raged the man again, "I've never even heard of them, where is it now?"

When the stranger said it was tied up in the back car park, money began to change hands like it was going out of fashion. It was just going dark as everyone piled out into the car park, and the two beasts unleashed. What followed can hardly be described, the noise of growling and barking filled the air, as blood and fur flew everywhere. Finally, a very sorry and dejected looking pit bull terrier came limping back up, one eye closed, ear hanging off --- a thoroughly beaten specimen.

"By the heck!" said the boaster, "My dog has never suffered a hiding like this in his life before. What did you say yours was called again?"

"A long nose, long tailed, short legged terrier." - - - - - said the quiet stranger, "Or some people call them crocodiles!"

GREAT GREAT GRANDFATHER

Some time ago I did what many Islanders have done, and that was to make a family tree. I spent hours on who married who and the names of their offspring, checking church records and visits to the Greffe office. I even visited the Priaulx library to see if we were entitled to a coat - of - arms.

Imagine my surprise when I received a letter from Somerset house, after checking on a mainland member of the lineage to be told:-

'Your great great grandfather met his untimely demise in 1857, when attending a public function. The platform on which he was standing gave way and he plunged to his death.'

Whatever way you look at it, you have got to admit that's a posh way to say he was hanged!

* * * * * * * * * * * *

QUICK THINKING

The quickest thinking I ever heard of was a man working in the French Halles. A little old lady came to the stall and asked;

"Do you think it would be possible for me to buy half a cabbage?"

"Half a cabbage?" repeated the man in disbelief. "Just a moment I'll have to ask the boss." He walked through to the back room and said, "You're never going to believe this boss, but there is some tight fisted old biddy out there wants to buy half a bloney cabbage." And then out of the corner of his eye he saw that the old lady had followed him through to see what the answer would be. So, quick as a flash he turned and said, "And this dear lady has offered to buy the other half!"

* * * * * * * * * * * *

CHAPTER FIFTEEN

THE HERMIT OF PLEINMONT

Because the article on Steve Piquet by Walter Clapham was so enjoyed in 'Donkey's Ears Ago' I have included this article by Kay Bragg in its entirety.

THE STORY OF STEVE PIQUET, ODDITY, INDIVIDUALIST.

By KAY BRAGG

I first met Steve Piquet --- 'the Hermit of Pleinmont' --- in the summer of 1960, while walking, one evening, along the coast road in the south west corner of the Island. Standing against the sea-wall was a short, tough-looking, unkempt man with a tanned, pugnacious face and silvery hair that blew wild in the wind. At his heels were five or six little dogs who at once got into a yelping, scrambling chase with Carlo, my landlady's black labrador, who was my only companion on these lonely walks.

I guessed that this must be the 'awful man' who inhabited a concrete bunker, relic of the German occupation, and of whom people had warned me. He was a surly character, they said, who used shocking language, scrounged off tourists and got paid by the States (the Island government) for tidying-up jobs that he never did, and drank heavily.

Understandably, therefore, I was wary of Steve, and he was suspicious of me, as most people --- for life, he told me later, had taught him to be on his guard. Nevertheless, something seemed to draw us together, if not at first into friendship, at least into a kind of alliance.

I had many chats with him in the following weeks. He had, I learned, been born in New Zealand of Guernsey - Jersey parentage and had once been a schoolteacher. However, deciding there was more money to be made in the ring, he had turned professional boxer and became well known in the Channel Isles in the 1920s. After that he had kept a shop, first at L'Eree on the west coast of Guernsey, and later in the town of St Peter Port.

Wanting to do something more purposeful than simply sell groceries and sweets. He had started clubs for the rugged, hard-to-handle sons of the west coast fishermen and growers, teaching the boys to box and 'keeping them out of trouble.' He carried on this youth work with very little funds, I gathered, and at times little encouragement.

The peak of his career as a sports organizer came during the German Occupation, when fed-up one day with watching a Nazi film three times, he marched into the cinema manager's office and persuaded him to start boxing contests. These did much to relieve the boredom of Guernsey's trapped male population during the war. And Steve, as an organizer and trainer, had been right at the centre of it all.

What had happened, then, to turn him into the hermit of Pleinmont? I never discovered the whole truth, for it was buried beneath layers of defensive and secret pain.

Perhaps it had all begun when he was a young man, for he spoke harshly of a girl who had deserted him during the First World War.

CURLY MARTIN

PETER 'MAD MAX' TROALIC

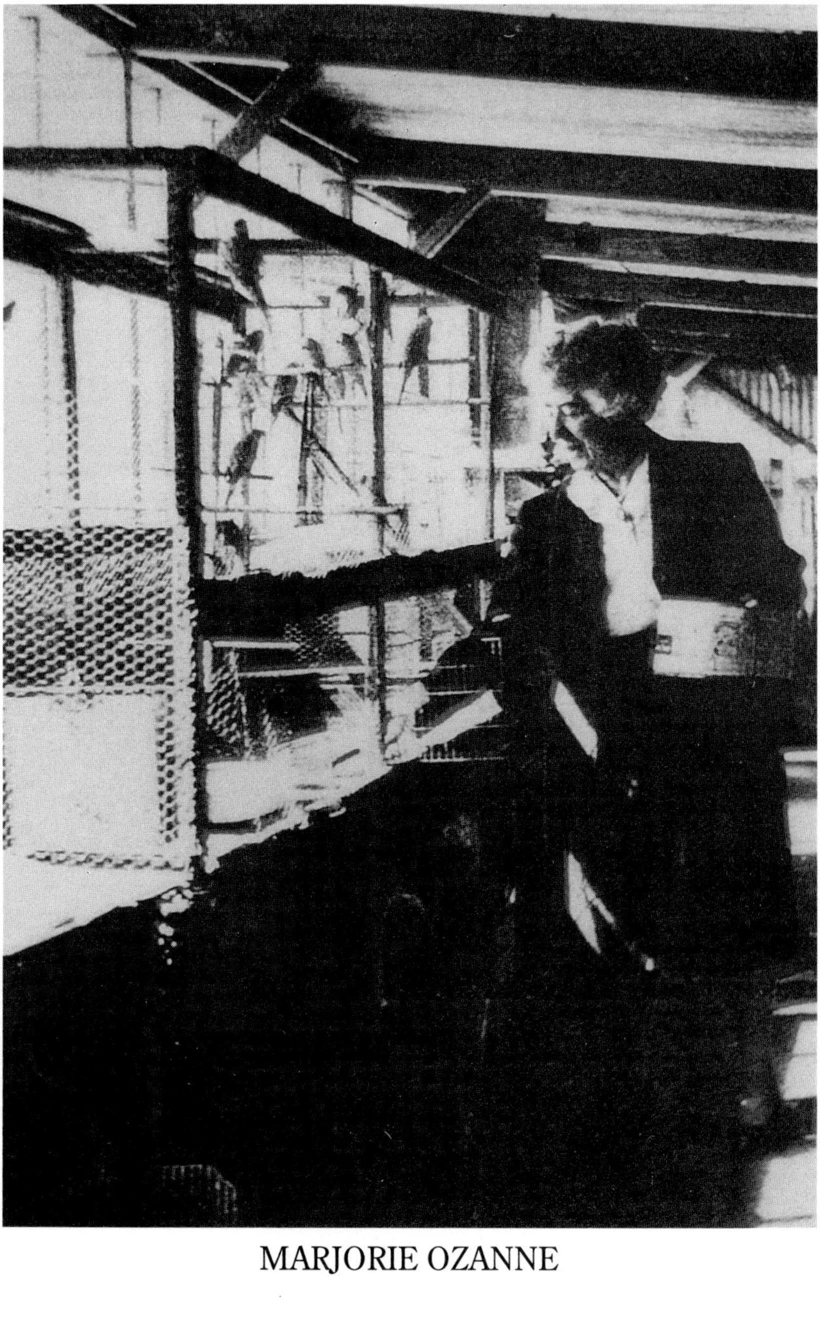

MARJORIE OZANNE

BONNIE NEWTON

PAUL LE MARQUAND

SAMMY JOHNSON

Clearly, though, he had always been independent and restless, drifting from one job to another, and his family in New Zealand had seldom heard from him. During the Occupation, running a sort of semi-resistance, semi-black market operation, with the help of his 'boys', gave him temporarily the feeling, for once, that he and the community were on the same side. But when peace came, people went back to their old ways, while Steve, his back injured as a result of imprisonment by the Germans, had to scrape for a living.

"People here forgot that me and my boys stole from the Germans to help feed them," he used to say bitterly.

Not everyone forgot Steve though, and certainly not his 'boys', for when he ran into housing difficulties after the war it was they -- by now grown men -- who converted the bunker into a home for him. Steve named it 'Onmeown.'

Most of my early talks with Steve Piquet took place as we clambered up and down cliffs and craggy hillsides. He made regular rounds, even in the worst weather and sometimes at great risk to himself, to make sure that his goats had not wandered into danger or hooked themselves up on their tethering ropes, and to look after the nannies when they were kidding. Often these expeditions were made at night, with only the light of Steves torch to guide us, and I would be left with Carlo, hanging precariously to some ledge, while Steve charged off into the night, bawling raucously : "Scrounger! Oxo! William!" He called all his goats by name, and one of the sights of Pleinmont was to see his herd clambering down the hillsides in answer to his bellow.

As I scrambled and tripped and caught my breath, I had the feeling that Steve was putting me through some kind of trial by ordeal to find out if I was just another one of 'them' or worthy to be his 'girl.' I must have passed the test for soon I was allowed to do something that few others had done in recent years, let alone strangers from England -- to go inside the bunker.

The invitation was given with typical Piquet gruffness. His back had been hurting him, so I offered to apply a plaster. "Well you'd better come inside then," he'd said, "But I don't want any sarcastic remarks!" I was careful not to make any, but the inside of 'Onmeown' was certainly a shock to me. I had expected that it would be pretty rough, but it was more like a closed-in rubbish dump.

When people heard that I had been inside the hermit's lair they put on anxious expressions, but I now knew that Steve was far from the coarse, loose-living character of popular legend (he really preferred chocolate to alcohol!). I knew, too, that he had begun to 'adopt' me and would no more have wanted to harm me than one of his beloved animals.

After this I began to call in regularly at the bunker, sitting surrounded by dogs listening to Steve talk by the flickering light of an oil-lamp (and, as it now seems, always against the background of 'Semprini's Serenade' coming from his cracked old radio). He told me many stories about his animals, for instance, how, during the Occupation, his bitch, Blackeye-who lay on my lap, a venerable lady of 19 --- had been stolen by a German Army cook for his stew-pot and, surprisingly, was recovered and returned to Steve by the Nazi police!

He also knew a number of yarns (picked up from the local people and no doubt improved upon where necessary) about the not-so-distant days when the west coast of the Island had been a smugglers' stronghold and the fishermen used to join with French trawler crews to outwit the customs men. Then there were his stories for summer visitors, in which the Island's forts, prehistoric dolmens and other relics acquired racy histories that would certainly have lifted astonished eyebrows at meetings of the learned Societe Guernesiaise.

On the other hand sometimes a dramatic story I thought Steve had made up would turn out to be true. For that was how he always was --- made up of an unpredictable mixture of directness and craftiness, candour and bluff, plain truthfulness and wild exaggeration.

People told me that my coming had made a great difference to Steve. He smiled more often and behaved less like a bear with a sore head. He shaved more frequently and dressed less like a tramp. He made grudging attempts, in response to my nagging, to clean up his bunker. He even came up warily for social evenings at the bungalow.

At the beginning of 1961, Steve had the first bad attack of the chest and lung trouble that was finally to kill him, and I did my best to nurse him through it. A favourite way of introducing me to people after that was: "This is Kay --- and *you've* no reason to thank her. If it wasn't for her, I'd have been out of your way long ago!" Steve was especially grateful that I saved him from having to go into hospital, for he was terrified of what would happen to his animals if he were taken away.

A landmark in my life was New Year's Eve, 1961. I had recently become sole tenant of the bungalow I had grown to love so much. So, as Steve's birthday was on January 1st. I decided to hold a combined house-warming, New Year's Eve and birthday party for Steve, inviting about 30 people. Steve was full of snorts and derisive remarks about it, but clearly was inwardly very pleased. He arrived -- much too early -- looking clean and trim with his hair neatly combed, and proved to be a great social success. It was his biggest step back so far into normal human society.

Winning the affection and protection of the hermit of Pleinmont had its drawbacks, however, for Steve -- the frustrated organizer -- had an interfering, domineering side to him that had made him quite a few enemies. I remember his overhearing a woman in a shop one day complaining about the price of a brush. "Go to Woolworths, madam, if you want a brush -- much better value there!" he informed her in a voice that could be heard by everyone. He was also apt to pounce on passing visitors and organize their day for them, telling them where they ought to go, where they ought to have tea, and even lecturing them for carrying too much paraphernalia! Most people took Steve's interference in good part, but others did not like having their customers sent elsewhere or being told how to run their lives. I resented it myself at times.

By now another influence besides mine was helping to draw Steve out of his seclusion. Following an appearance on television in a programme about Guernsey, the hermit had become a tourist attraction. Hundreds of visitors came to Pleinmont looking for him and the bunker and the goats. Being a celebrity helped him financially, because most of the visitors gave him something after chatting to him or taking his photograph: many, too, took a liking to him and were fascinated by his way of life and would write to him afterwards. But there was another type who would ignore the 'Private' notice outside the bunker and come right up to the entrance, staring in as if it were a zoo. Some of them even carried off flowers and bits of stone from his little garden as souvenirs. As his health failed, Steve found this continual invasion of his privacy a great strain.

Steve fell ill again that summer. He was found semi-conscious in the road by some men, who came to fetch me. This time there was no help for it, he had to go to hospital.

The fate of his dogs and goats worried him much more than his own condition, and I promised to try to look after them. This meant feeding seven dogs besides Carlo (alas, the parting proved too much for Blackeye, now 21, who grieved and died), and trying to act as goatherd to a wandering flock of 47. Despite warnings from the authorities, Steve had allowed his original few goats to multiply into a large herd, many of them wild and untethered, his story being that strays had 'joined' his private herd.

As it happened, what ended Steve's stay in hospital was a great goat crisis, which was headlined in the Guernsey press and brought him to the tv screen again. The authorities --- increasingly uneasy because of complaints that the goats were roaming far and wide, damaging property -- struck suddenly. The police swooped and rounded up all the goats of Pleinmont and took them to the States' slaughterhouse. Steve, still in hospital, was warned to go and identify his private herd or else they would be destroyed together with the wild goats.

Though still not well, he rushed to the slaughterhouse, argued and pleaded and ranted: and eventually, with the aid of the publicity he received, managed to find homes for all the goats that he could not afford to register officially as his own. Those few days saw Steve at his most formidable, fighting tooth and nail to save living creatures from destruction. His action won him many new friends in the Island and on the mainland -- and also, by an odd chance, the admiration of a man thousands of miles away, an American businessman living in California, himself an animal-lover, who read the story of Steve's efforts to save his goats in a newspaper. He wrote him a warm and sympathatic letter, never expecting to get a reply, and was delighted to receive a letter from the Guernsey hermit describing his life. The correspondence continued and developed into a close friendship, the American sending Steve gifts of money now and then to help him feed his animals.

The two men were looking forward to meeting, as Steve's friend planned to make a European tour and stay a few days in Guernsey. But the trip had to be postponed and by the time the American reached Guernsey Steve was dead.

Fortunately, Steve had a few happy weeks back at Pleinmont, perhaps his happiest for many years, before returning to hospital for the last time. A group of his friends made it possible for him to come home by clearing out and burning all the rubbish in 'Onmeown' -- a job that took them two exhausting days -- and then painting and sprucing up the whole place.

Steve himself stepped out of the ambulance looking fresh and clean in a white shirt and yellow pullover -- 'like a ruddy daffodil,' he snorted. Channel Television arrived to record the joyful reunion with his dogs, among them Carlo whose great affectionate leaps finally laid the old man on his back!

Many people in the Island undoubtedly felt a deep sense of loss when they heard last August that the hermit of Pleinmont was no more. As Steve had died without enough money for a proper funeral and burial a collection was organized and about 150 people -- some of them far from well-off themselves --- contributed. A rough granite headstone was inscribed 'Buried by his friends.'

Much as I still love the rocky coastline and fern-covered hillsides of Pleinmont, this beautiful spot is now -- and always will be for me --- short of an extra surge of life which Steve Piquet brought to it.

CHAPTER SIXTEEN

CONCLUSION

All too soon the time has come around again. We didn't get a chance to talk of all the characters we could have.

One was, twenty five years Jerbourg Newsboy, Dereck, who finally had to quit, with the closing of the Le Hurays, old mill cafe and paper shop.

We could have remembered the water-polo matches in the careening hard, near the old flat states barge with the winch in the middle. The marvellous floodlit galas at the ladies pool, when after dark all the floodlights were put out, the water was set on fire, and Hayward Quevatre would do a perfect swallow dive right through the flames.

I could have told you about the days when Ted joined us around the stove and his stories about coming back to the Island after the war, with all the other youths of his age. How they found a German half-track vehicle in the tunnels near Rouge Rue, and one of the lads who was learning his trade as a mechanic managed to get it going. They all piled on to it as it was driven through the tunnel and out into the sunshine looking like they were all taking part in a victory parade.

He made late forty five and early forty six sound like great years in which to be a teenager, especially when he recounted the time he and his mates rowed out to Brehon tower, and found it exactly as the last German garrison had left it. A full size snooker table complete with balls and cues, and a full size bar complete with optics and bottles. They spent quite a few happy days out there before someone else stumbled on it, and spoiled everything.

I could have shared with you what finally convinced Barry (Stans nipper) to give up the drink. He said that he regained consciousness one morning in the bottom of a shaft. As he lay there with his head banging and his throat all parched he could see fluffy clouds passing the top of the shaft. Barry-boy he thought, you've gone too far this time, you've either fallen down a disused mine shaft or dried out well. As he lay there looking up he began to wiggle his fingers to see if his arms were broken, then he began wiggling his toes to check on his legs. Then his conscience began to trouble him. Look at the mess the booze has got you into, how on earth have you fallen in here. Finally he picked up the courage to sit up and check out the situation, only to find he was at a mates house, laying in the fireplace looking up the chimney.

We could have discussed the standard of education required for the police force following a report that a policeman once found a dead horse outside of Luckies shop, and then dragged it all the way up to Elm Grove because he couldn't spell Gibauderie.

Ah well, I suppose I'll have to go, me.

A LA PROCHAINE.

OTHER BOOKS BY THE SAME AUTHOR

'Donkey's Ears Ago' . . . . . November 1996